WHY YOU CRYING?

MY LONG, HARD LOOK
AT LIFE, LOVE, AND
LAUGHTER

GEORGE LOPEZ

with
Armen
Keteyian

A TOUCHSTONE BOOK
PUBLISHED BY SIMON & SCHUSTER
NEW YORK   LONDON   TORONTO   SYDNEY

TOUCHSTONE
Rockefeller Center
1230 Avenue of the Americas
New York, NY 10020

For information regarding special discounts for bulk purchases,
please contact Simon & Schuster Special Sales at 1-800-456-6798
or business@simonandschuster.com

Designed by William Ruoto

Manufactured in the United States of America

1 3 5 7 9 10 8 6 4 2

Library of Congress Cataloging-in-Publication Data
Lopez, George.
Why you crying? : my long, hard look at life, love, and laughter /
George Lopez with Armen Keteyian.
p.   cm.
"A Touchstone book."
1. Lopez, George.   2. Comedians—United States—Biography.
3. Television actors and actresses—United States—Biography.
I. Keteyian, Armen.   II. Title.
PN2287.L633A3   2004
792.702'8'092—dc22   [B]   2004045404

ISBN 0-7432-5994-7

To the woman who saved me from myself: my lovely wife, Ann. And to my beautiful daughter, Mayan.

—GL

To the three singular women in my life: Dede, Kristen, and KELLY (who requested all CAPS), and my late father, Albert, a most honorable man.

—AK

CONTENTS

CONTENTS

viii

WHY YOU CRYING?

WHY YOU CRYING?

I must confess . . . I'm a crying mess.

A newly crowned Miss America, a Barbara Walters interviewee, your average second grader, they have *nada* on me.

Now, don't get the wrong idea. I'm not . . . NOT a blubbering fool or the kind of guy who cries at weddings. The tears I shed are often private. I cry sometimes thinking about the father I never knew, the mother I never really had. I break up thinking about how long I lived on the defensive—never smiling, never comfortable with myself or my body. I cry over the loss of the comic genius Freddie Prinze Sr. and the physical suffering of Richard Pryor. I still tear up at the thought of seeing my grandfather—the only real man in my life—laid out in the funeral home. I cry, believe me, *I cry,* over my deeply dysfunctional family.

My grandmother, Benita Gutierrez, inspired the title of this book.

"Come over here. Why you crying? Why you crying? No, tell me for real. Why you crying?"

"Because you hit me."

"Liar, I barely touched you. You want me to hit you for real, cabrón? You want me to HIT YOU FOR REAL? Mira, you can't even touch him because right away, he starts crying, hombre. Mr. Sensitive."

Actually, she's done more than inspire the title. My grandmother is the essence of my entire stand-up act and television show. She was hilarious and she didn't even know it; it was her attitude. I didn't know comedy could come so cold and often so cruel. She was—no other word does it justice—just *mean*. Her sarcasm ran deep. Like when I was I don't remember how old, and I asked, "Where do babies come from?" and she said, "Whores. Now go play."

You know the saddest fucking thing? One day I found a picture at the house of me and my high school girlfriend with her arms around me. I weighed about 175 pounds at the time, damn near what I do now, having dropped 50 large over the last year. But all I can remember from those days is how *fat* I felt, and how every fucking ounce of that godawful feeling was fed day in and day out by my grandmother. How could I be like that? Be that tall and that thin and still feel like I weighed 300 pounds?

I became a comedian as a way to cope with this kind of wretched psychological abuse, a life so sad it had to be funny. These days, I'm using all the tears and heartbreak to make folks laugh. Over the past two years I've sent tens of thousands into gales of laughter, ripping up places one hundred times the size of the clubs I bombed in during the early nineties, otherwise known as the I Hate Me years when I was the Angriest Most Depressed Man Alive. Didn't have a manager, an agent, or much of a life, a stray cat on the loose, drowning my sorrows in alcohol, undone by the fact I had become what I swore to myself I never would: a nobody.

You see, I'm as tragic as anyone out there. Maybe a little more so. As a little boy, I grew up angry, alone, teased, and tormented. I grew up around Nobodies as a Nobody wanting to be something else. And that's as true a statement as I've ever said.

And now, after twenty-four years of struggle on the stand-up circuit, I'm swimming in the mainstream. I have a family sitcom on ABC television, which has turned out to be the first Latino-based prime-time hit since the early 1970s when Freddie Prinze Sr. starred on *Chico and the Man.* My show, *George Lopez,* is powering into its fourth season on ABC, a lifetime for Latinos on network TV. In it I play what could have been—the manager at an airplane parts factory married to a sassy wife with two challenging kids and a mother only my grandmother would love. Hailed by critics as a cross-cultural success (our audience, on average, is nearly 90 percent non-Hispanic), we regularly dominate the twelve-to-forty-nine-year-old demographic coveted by advertisers.

So, yeah, I'm a crier. There are tears of sadness and tears of joy, tears of pain and tears of heartache. And these days? Tears of gratitude and tears of triumph. Yeah, I've cried every last one of those babies, and I'm not ashamed to admit it.

To me, tears are tiny drops of remembrance, portals to the past. They bleach the dirty laundry of my life. They're my release. A sign I'm alive. That's why people have tears in their eyes when they laugh, because the humor hits them deep in a place that's harsh but real. When I'm onstage doing my thing, the audience and I are connecting to our individual embarrassments and pain. But this time, the tears let us know that we've moved on. That we're strong enough to meet on the most intimate of terms, allowing someone into your heart.

Well, welcome to *my* heart.

Why you crying? No, tell me for real.

ON TO YOU

No matter what the Secret Service says, I swear I didn't steal it, man. Why is it when something's missing, the first face people look for is . . . brown?

Okay, so I did have it in my possession. In my jacket. After the president of the United States of America had already left the stage . . . Oh, all right, I took it.

What can I tell you? It was a once-in-a-lifetime moment: March 2003. I'm up on stage performing for the pleasure of George W. Bush and his wife, Laura. It was probably the most important gig a stand-up comic could ever have, and I was a little unsure. Trouble was, I didn't think that much of my act would work in Washington. Now, at The Ice House in Pasadena or the Improv, say, in Brea, no problem. I'd come out, like always, decked out in a suit, no intro, just my signature song, WAR's "Low Rider" pumping through the speakers, and start right in.

"The Chicano? Man, Chicanos are their own breed. Even though we're born in the United States, we still have accents. I know, huh. I know, eh. You think we're from Canada. I knew, eh. Tell 'em, eh.

We add words that aren't there. We make up words. Other people say, 'Are you going?' Chicanos say, 'Hey, are you going, or not?' Or not? And how many times have you been in the store and your mom's yelling, 'Mijo, is this what you wanted—or what?' Or what?

"Or, 'How long you guys been here?' 'We berly got here.' 'I just arrived, eh.' 'I'm berly here ten minutes, eh?' Berly?

"They never let you get too confident—that's the mentality of the Mexican family. You know, you use a big word and right away, 'Hey, cómo está?' 'Ah, I got a new job and I have to go to Orientation.' 'Oh, you're the big man now. Toilet paper on your shoe, cabrón. Caca hand. Orien-tay-shun.' "

But at the historic Ford Theatre in Washington, DC, I was dealing with an entirely different group of people. I guess you could call it diverse. Out of the six-hundred-person crowd, there were about two hundred white people, three hundred really white people, and about a hundred people so white they were pink. The only Latinos within ten miles were either carrying trays or parking cars.

But you know what, I just went for it. I was wearing a tux and a shit-eating grin and charming the pants right off all those *Republicanos.*

"You know," I said, "in the latest census, Latinos are the largest minority." Complete silence from the audience. "Thank you—I'll take your silence as confirmation. I'm kinda surprised, though. We're so hard to count. *We never open our doors. Why would someone be knocking—what have we done? Now, if you honk, we come out. The Chicano doorbell—two blasts from the horn.*

"And then, of course, we lie during the census. 'How many live in this house?' 'Oh, just two.' Two? We're known for converting the garage and renting it out. It's a selling point—how many people have a remote-control front door?

"So many of us are starting to vote now that someday soon there's going to be a Latino in the White House," I continued, heading toward my best punch line of the night.

"Of course, we plan on leaving it white . . . with just a little blue trim."

That Ford crowd was rolling in the aisles. And there were the president and Mrs. Bush, dead center, laughing. They're into it.

By the end of the evening I'm feeling good, real *goood,* as the

Navy Choir comes out to join me and the eve-
ning's other performers—singers Brian McKnight,
Michele Lee, LeAnn Rimes—onstage. Counting
their sixty, we've got about seventy people up standing around when a worker appears and sets a piece of
masking tape on the floor. Next thing you know here
comes the podium and the velvet blue presidential seal, followed by
this announcement:

"Ladies and gentlemen, President George W. Bush and Mrs.
Bush."

Now the Man is no more than a foot and a half away, eighteen
inches in front of me. Probably the closest any Chicano I know has
ever got to this kind of power without saying, "More coffee, Mr. President?" And I can see he has got a little speech typed out and I can actually *see my name* on the sheet. The name I hated growing up as a kid.

I'm thinking, *Well, that's a nice little keepsake, an artistic artifact.* So
when the president finishes thanking us, and God blessing America,
and the choir reaches a crescendo, I make a spontaneous move. I
swipe the speech and slyly Bond it into my jacket.

Later, in the car on our way to the post party, I show my wife,
Ann, my memento of the evening. Well, let me tell you, she screamed,
"Oh, my God!" like I was George *Clooney* or something . . .

My personal pleasure lasted as long as it took for bandleader
Tom Scott to find me.

"The White House is on to you, man."

"Get the fuck out of here," I said.

"I wish I were kidding," said Scott, "but I'm not."

"What is this?" I laughed. "A *Miami Vice* episode? Who uses the
term *on to you?*"

Evidently Tom did, going on to say, "There's been a theft at the
Ford Theatre, and you can expect a visit from the Secret Service."

"How would they know I have it?" I said. "There were a lot of
people up there onstage. Why do I have it? Because I'm Mexican?"

"I'm just telling you what they said to me," said Scott.

"Well," I said, "I'm just going to tell them I don't have it."

Ten seconds later an agent from the Secret Service shows up over my right shoulder. He was all the way to "Mr. Lopez, I'm from the Secret Service and we'd like to speak with you" before I cracked like an egg and yelled, "It's in the car! I'll show you!"

I took the guy by the arm, apologizing all the way outside, barely hearing his offer of regrets, blah, blah, insisting it was standard operating procedure for all presidential papers to be passed on to the archives. (How could I have been so *stupid*? Of course, the presidential *archives!*)

There was only one problem: There were about fifty identical black Town Cars in the parking lot, each and every one populated with a sleeping driver. I shook a few of them awake without luck before Secret Service Guy considered the odds and told me he would see me after the party.

"How will I find you?" I asked.

"Don't worry," he answered, "I'll find you."

And, of course, he did.

"Excuse me," I said, after I'd handed him the speech and he was leaving. "How did you find out it was me?"

"We actually went to the TV production truck and reviewed the last forty-five minutes of the show scene by scene, and we had the shot of the podium enlarged.

"You know," he added as he smiled and walked off into the night, "my money was on Michele Lee."

Funny. For most of my sad, tormented life I never had any stories like this to tell. I was always talking about other people. Now I've got a big one.

I guess you could say people are on to me.

When I was a kid, I had a horrible self-image. That's what happens in my world when you've got a huge head and lips to match, and your skin is so dark your friends' parents won't let their kids play with you. Those friends—and I use that word lightly—used to call me nigger.

Anglo kids, man, they get great nicknames like Skip or Chauncey or Muffy or Honey or Cutie. Our nicknames are Gordo or Feo, if you're lucky enough to be both fat and ugly. Chino was for the slanty eyed, Flaco for the skinny, Beaver for the buckteeth. Whatever was wrong with you, that became your nickname. That can't be good. Take it from me, when you're known as Rockhead or Spuds, it has a tendency to destroy your self-esteem, as do the beatings that often accompany the taunts.

Finally, one day when I was about ten, I'd had enough. I was up in Yolo, a small town near Sacramento, and this big fat kid named Rango was fucking with me. I'd never really fought back before, always swallowing the shit. But on the front steps of the local library, something hit me and I hit Rango. Swinging as hard and fast as I could, I knocked Rango down and kept on punching and punching. I kicked his *ass*. After that, he was nice.

Today I have what you might call a *disarming* look—but people relate to my realness. Face it, I'm never going to be confused with Tom Cruise—or even Tom Arnold—but I think I have a look that endears people to me. Fans or people who meet me for the first time say I seem like a real person. Guess what? I am. But I didn't appreciate my unique looks back then.

I remember this one time, we went to Disneyland. Now, of course we never visited the Magic Kingdom like normal people. Never went with friends or family members on normal days or nights. No, we'd go on Gas Night or RCA Night.

So this one night we go, and I really want the Mickey Mouse hat with the ears where they embroider your name.

I told my grandmother, "I want the hat with ears."

You know what she told me?

"One, you're lucky we brought you. Two, you want a souvenir—save your ticket. And three, your ears stick out more than the fuckin' hat. Here, I'll just write your name across your forehead."

The first time I remember getting a compliment I was thirteen years old, and it didn't come from anyone in my family but from an African-American saleslady behind a jewelry counter at the Montgomery Ward in Panorama City.

"My God," she said. "You have the most beautiful lips I've ever seen in my life."

WHAAT?

"And your skin is such a beautiful color."

Okay, now I'm thinking, is this some kind of sick Monkey Ward joke they play on Mexican kids? You know, pick out the sorriest-ass-looking *cabrón* in the whole store, make him smile, and win a weekend in Vegas. Thing is, the lady was straight up.

The next time I got a compliment, of sorts, was from Cindy Coronado right out of high school. How's that for a name? Man, she was beautiful. Her parents actually owned their own business, an upholstery store, which to a Mexican is like owning a national bank. Cindy got dropped off at school in a Cadillac, the whole deal, and she was so fine that my friend Arnold and I used to go to Thrifty's and buy shit we didn't even need just because she worked behind the register.

So one night at a party she'd been drinking and I ended up with her. We went out for a while, and one evening on the phone she says to me, "Why do you put yourself down so much?"

And I'm like, *WHAAT?*

"You're so nice and sweet, and it gets to me that you put yourself down so much."

And you know what? She was right. I was degrading myself for no other reason than to try and make her laugh. For years I did that. For years I made fun of myself. For years I was the punch line.

DIFFERENT PEOPLES

People ask me, does it matter if someone calls you a Mexican, Latino, or Hispanic? I don't mind Mexican or Chicano, which is a Mexican-American, but Hispanic I don't like. The U.S. Census Bureau came up with it, and who wants to be associated with a word that has panic in it? Of course, in a way, it's progress: In the seventies, we used to be Other.

Ultimately, we're all Americans (even the undocumented ones), and we have a lot in common. But we really are different peoples. Take language, as an example. Chicanos have one of their own. Something I like to call Spanglish.

GLOSSARY OF SPANGLISH TERMS

A and **O.** Anal and Oral. We use it like Anglos use XXOO.

A.T.M. Not a place to get quick cash. A Toda Madre means "Bitchin'." "Hope your summer is A Toda Madre."

Buey. Dumb Ass. It has become a greeting: "Qué pasó, Buey?" = "What's going on, dude?"

Cabrón. Son of a bitch, or worse, depending on the inflection. "Take me to the store, cabrón." Take it from me, it works.

Chulo. Good-looking. Not a Cinnamon Stick. The best is to be called a Papi Chulo: Sweet Daddy!

Culo. Ass, backside. Needs no further explanation. But I'll give you one: "What's going on? It smells like Culo in here." Response: "Nahhing."

Dale Gas. Give it the gas, go for it! "I'm coming over to the house. Dale Gas."

Ese. Not a literary composition. It's homeboy. "Qué pasó, ese?" = "What's up, homeboy?"

Feo. Ugly, Not Very Attractive. A popular nickname for kids. "Feo, go get me another beer."

Flaco. Skinny or Fat. A 300-pound uncle is always Flaco.

Gente. People. You want to get in the club but too many Gente. Let's go through the kitchen. Who's going to stop Mexicans going through the kitchen? Works every time.

Gordo. Chubby. Our nicknames are always the shit that's wrong with us. "Gordito, tuck your shirt in."

Joto. Gay or of Questionable Manhood. When you're not crazy about someone. You don't even need a reason. "Look at the way he walks. Joto."

Mamón. Suck-Up or Kiss-Ass. "Can I help you, Mamón?!"

Más Chingón. Bad Ass. The Man. Carlos Santana is "El Más Chingón."

Mendijo. Fool or Slow-Minded. He forgot to put the radiator cap on. Mendijo.

Pendejo. Stupid. The Absolutely Most Popular Put-down. When I tore my Achilles tendon, my grandmother said, "Por Pendejo . . . ," because I was so stupid.

Puto. Like joto, means gay. But it has become the most popular greeting, somehow. "Long time no see, Puto." "Good to see you too, Puto."

También. Also; include me. "That Chick is Fine . . . También!!!"

Vato. Dude; Guy; Man. "Qué Pasó, Vato?" Vato Loco = "Crazy Dude."

We're just different people. We never say congratulations when people do well. Other people send balloons and plants: "Oh, my God, I just heard, Megan. Congrats. Totally cool. Awesome. You totally need to be district manager. You're—oh, my God, I'm like so happy for you."

Us? Silence.

"Hey, did you hear I got a job over at the hospital?"

"S'about time."

Do we say good luck? Never. No, we say, "Hey, don't fuck it up like the last time." *Or,* "So now you think you're all bad, or what?"

Yeah, go to the Hallmark store and look for that card.

"Hi, can I help you?"

"Yeah, you don't have a Now-You-Think-You're-All-Bad card?"

When the show was first picked up, some people at ABC sent me a plant. I said, "What is this, a fucking joke? You're gonna send a Mexican a plant? We don't water enough and cut enough grass and you're going to send me a plant! How about a six-pack of Corona, cabrones?" *How about that? A fuckin' plant.*

Latinos are just different. When we raise kids, our first instinct is just no.

"Mom?"

"No!"

My grandmother, all she said was no.

"Grandma?"

"No."

"You don't even know what it is."

"I know what's not."

Kids these days talk back, man, they talk BACK. I never

talked back. You see Anglo kids in the store. "No, I won't."

"Now you listen to me, Dakota. I'm the parent here. You will. Believe me. Do you want a gold star when you get home, Dakota? Because you're going—you won't get *The Lion King* on DVD. You're not. Do you want a consequence?"

I love going to the stores and seeing parents actually get down on one knee. "Can you understand me, Tyler? This behavior is inappropriate. Well, I need to apologize to you because I was using my outdoor voice inside."

My grandmother was old-school. She would pick me up. "Vámonos, cabrón, we're going. Mira, cómo no, que no. Vamos. Mira, you don't want to go. Bullshit, you're going. Mira, well, you know what, wait in the fucking car. Wait in the car. Wait in the car! Why you crying? Why you crying? Well, roll down the window so you can breathe."

And if you look at the news, only white mothers have ever been arrested for hitting their kids. Amateurs. Amateurs.

Us, we see the camera. "Mira, the camera's there. I know, mira, talk, talk, porque when we get home. Mira, dance. Do it all. Throw yourself on the ground. Throw yourself. Because when I get you home, cabrón, I can already feel it in my hand."

You know what my grandmother would do? My grandmother would go get a shirt. "Mira, come, son of a bitch. We're going to try this on. Mira, vámonos, cabrón. Vamos, mira. Can we borrow the fitting room for one second?" *And then she would beat the shit out of me in the fitting room. WHAP!*

And the salespeople would be all happy when we came out. "How did everything turn out?"

It didn't.

And the other thing is about Mexican people, man, we don't respond to authority.

There can be a yellow line, and white people will say,

"Excuse me, can you stay behind the yellow line?"

"Oh, my God, I'm sooo sorry. I didn't read the sign. Oh, my God. Kevin, can you stay behind the yellow line? This man was nice enough to alert us to the fact that he wants us behind the line."

And then that white person becomes the monitor. "Hi, I'm sorry, I don't know you, but can you stay behind the yellow line? This gentleman kindly asked that we all remain behind the line. Fantastic. Our kids go to the same school?"

Mexicans, we cross.

"Excuse me, sir, can you stay behind that yellow line?"

"Fuck you. Hey, make me go behind that yellow line. Make me. I'm right here, bitch. Call the cops. Go ahead. I'm right here."

Another thing about Mexican dudes, man, we never move out. White kids, first chance they get they're out the door to college or some exotic European backpacking trip or some shit. Us? We live at home forever. We don't even have a key. "Ey, mamá, leave the kitchen door open . . . be late." That's why in Los Angeles you see very few Latino homeless. Because you gotta leave home to be homeless.

And if we do move out, we move in with our aunt.

"You know, I went to your house, man. What happened?"

"I haven't been there for like three months, ese. My car's there because it don't run, pero I don't live there."

"Where do you live?"

"Shit, I live with my aunt. Mi tía. I'm in the garage, ese, they converted." Which to Mexicans means they pulled the car out.

And we die with no wills. White people die, they go to a law office all cordial. "Jonathan? Did I get the house? Tell me now. I did? Fantastic."

You can't get old Mexican people to make out a will because they're superstitious. "No, mira, hombre, it's like a reservation to die, *cabrón*. So you can take my things."

Mexican people never say they're sorry. My grandmother when I was young hit me with her car. I was in the driveway—I think she saw me— pang!

"You know where I park, *cabrón*. *Mira*, look where the oil is. Look at the showoff! Walk right. *Mira*, walk right! You wanna go to McDonald's? Okay. Then walk right. You want a Happy Meal? Then get fucking happy, *cabrón*."

Did she say she was sorry? What did she say? "Sorry, *'tá loco*. He's seven. I'm not going to say sorry. When he starts paying the bills, *cabrón*, then I'll say sorry."

You can go to dinner and some people save seats. "Oh, my God, is Shawn coming? Let's save a seat. Here, lemme put my sweater on the seat. This is for Shawn. Don't sit there cuz this is Shawn's seat. He just called on his cell phone. He's coming. He's running a little late."

And when they see him, they wave. "Shawn, oh, my God. Call him on his cell phone. Hi, Shawn! Oh, my God, I'm totally in front of you."

Mexicans, we look. "Ah, fuck, look who's over there. *Hide the chair.* Hide the chair. *Don't look over there!* Don't look over there. *Pretend we're talking. He saw? Shit. He saw me? Say, 'Swear to God.' Swear to God?* Yeah, come on. Fuck, you saw me, might as well."

Now before you get all bent out of shape and go off and call the local ACLU chapter, the Gay/Lesbian Alliance, or La Raza, relax. Check out the crowds at one of my shows first. Yes, I'm harsh. Yes, I'm putting my own people down. But it's true, and I'm also pushing empowerment. And, really, if we can't laugh at ourselves and others, who's left?

To Have Not

I was born on April 23, 1961, in a general hospital in East Los Angeles to a twenty-year-old wild, mixed-up streak of a girl named Frieda. Her migrant-worker husband stuck around for the entire first two *months* of my life. His first name was Anatasio and he disappeared one day without a trace taking my birth certificate and baby clothes with him, so it's not like I went to bed with a picture of him under my pillow, wishing he would come home. He was a thin, light-skinned Mexican with fine chiseled features and the last name of Lopez, and even today I'm not completely sure he was my father. What I am sure of is, I hated his last name. Hated that every kid in my immediate family was either Gutierrez or Hernandez—and I'm the one and only Lopez. I wanted to use the other family surnames, but they wouldn't let me. "No way. *Lopez.* That's your name," they said, "and you're gonna keep it." Maybe that's why from my very first thought I never felt like I belonged.

I don't want to sound like I'm auditioning for *Oprah,* but I don't think there was ever a moment in my childhood when I felt it was great to be a part of a family. Not a single one. It was awful to not have. Not have money, happiness, warmth, love, attention, or affection. Just awful.

Imagine: No pictures of me as a baby. No family albums brimming with photos of me rocking gently in a porch swing or opening presents at Christmas, a day rarely if ever celebrated. No shots of the

first day of school or my christening. No birthday parties for just me. Only combined ones. If my birthday was close enough to a baptism, my grandmother would say, "Jorge, this is your party, *también*. Why you crying? Mingle. *We'll get you a present when they're not looking, cabrón. Mira, mingle.*"

For the most part, the first six or seven years of my life are untraceable. I didn't exist photographically until I was seven or eight years old, and you know what? I never smiled in any of the shots. School picture? No smile. Team photo? No smile. A kid with dimples who doesn't smile? How sad is that? I asked my grandmother once why there were so few photos.

"Hey, I have pictures of you as a kid. All I need is four more shots and I can develop the roll."

Forty-three years, four pictures to go.

Hard as I try, I can't conjure up a single pleasant thought or happy memory of my mom. No smell of wildflowers in her hair or the sun streaming through the kitchen window while she baked cookies, dressed in a colorful apron. If I was talking to one of those police sketch artists and asked to describe the drive-by female in my life, she would look something like this: five feet six, dark hair, jumpy, uptight, along the lines of the Lily Tomlin character Ernestine. I can still smell her body odor.

Incorrigible. That's the word that comes to mind.

Frieda, man, she was trouble right from the start. She grew up with epilepsy and somehow managed to fall out of a moving car at thirteen. Yeah, you read that right. A *moving* car. It messed her up, man. She was never right after that, prone to these sudden horrible seizures. There we'd be, Mom and I talking by ourselves in the kitchen or hanging wash on the line and suddenly she'd collapse and have a fit. I was little. Didn't know what to do. And after screaming for a grandparent who wasn't around, I just stood or sat and watched the convulsions until, magically, thankfully, they'd stop as suddenly as they'd started, and she'd snap out of it.

She was a deeply troubled woman, going so far as to slash her wrists at one point. She ended up in Camarillo State Hospital. I'll never forget those Sunday drives. North up the coast along scenic Highway 101 toward beautiful Santa Barbara, the deep blue Pacific Ocean to the left, majestic mountains far off to the right. We'd always take the same exit, our car growing ever quieter as we neared the destination. I can still see the stark white walls, Frieda sitting in the chair zoned out on drugs, sedated like a zombie. Sundays with Mom. In the nuthouse.

Given her condition, she never really went to school and was pretty much a functional illiterate. Let me tell you, when you're a kid and out with your mom and someone asks her to sign and she can't, and she puts an X, well . . .

Frieda was a scammer from the get-go. She'd talk her way into things and talk her way out. She was the kind of woman who would leave the house at noon and be back by three with a TV. How she got it, nobody knew.

She was also an equal opportunity opportunist. Everybody who came by the house, whether it was the ice cream man or the Helm's bakery guy, my mom would hit him up for what she liked to call "credit," operating an "interest only" payment plan. Meaning her only interest was in never paying you back. She'd stiff everyone. I would be three blocks away on Maclay and the ice cream man would say, "Tell your mom she owes me $7.45." Right in front of my friends. That hurt.

My mom also displayed spectacularly bad taste in men. One time when I was about eight we ran away from home and found ourselves hitchhiking on the 5 Freeway, only to end up in a seedy downtown hotel with two guys trying to "be with" my mom. I don't even

want to remember how we escaped that mess. Another time she was working at this center for the disabled and she brought a guy home. He had one leg and a tube in his dick. His name was Gil. There is NOTHING more embarrassing than your mom wheeling a dude with one leg and a piss bag to Open House at your school. When you don't have a father, don't know your father, and your mom's wheeling Gil in . . . you don't know whether to laugh or cry. Most often you just hide.

And it just wasn't Gil. Oh, no. My mom had a whole menagerie of weird friends. One time we're staying at this apartment on Hubbard in the Valley and I wake up, music blasting, and I rub the sleep from my eyes to see dear ol' Mom on top of the dining room table, dancing in her bra and panties—everybody encouraging her to take it *all* off.

That was Mom—a party girl with great chichis and no parental instincts whatsoever. Parenting? You might as well have asked my mom to design the space shuttle. When I was ten, she bought me *Playboy* to pass the time on a bus trip to Sacramento. Today, kids get Harry Potter. I got Miss June. The fact is she had no interest in my welfare.

Around that time, she was dating this guy who was about forty years older, a Senior Citizen who lived in Yolo. She'd travel back and forth all the time, and one day, she just never came back. She eventually married the guy and had two daughters who consider themselves my sisters. Well, I don't. I rarely saw my mom and those kids after she remarried. To me, if you're not there at the beginning, you're not there at the end. And, to be honest, I have no interest in seeing them today.

Turns out when I was born it was well-known that my mother wasn't going to stick around and raise me. There was no long argument or deep family debate. She was in no condition to take care of herself, let alone anyone else. When I was around four, someone told my grandmother that they saw me walking in the street without any pants on, so she went to my mom's house and took me home. I was shuttled back and forth, but by the time I was ten she left for good and I got passed permanently over to my grandparents.

Lucky me.

Now, in some cultures, when a grandmother returns to the role of motherhood, the grandson or granddaughter is showered with attention and affection, nurtured day and night in the most love-filled atmosphere imaginable. From there the grateful child flourishes and ends up winning the Nobel Prize in literature, or at least managing a McDonald's.

Let's be clear here: That was not me.

Today, as millions of you know, my show explores the twisted, tortured relationship I share with my mother, standing in for my real-life grandmother. On the show, she's played by the wonderful actress Belita Moreno, and we engage in a constant war of words with me repeatedly and often unsuccessfully trying to wring a tiny drop of praise or affection from a woman seemingly incapable of expressing either emotion. It turns out to be much funnier on TV.

I used to call my grandmother "OLD" all the time, and maybe that's because Benita Gutierrez took an old-world approach where everything is bad and everyone untrusting. Positive emotion simply does not flow in her bloodstream. Her DNA Does Not Allow for praise or affection. To this day, she has never said she is proud of me. Never. Not once expressed happiness for my success in life.

You'd think at the end of all our shows when I come out onstage and bask in the applause and affection from the studio audience, you'd think my grandmother would be in the front row, hands held high, clapping to beat the band. Not mine. "If I would have known it was going to last this long," she said, "I wouldn't have come."

When Ann and I told her we were expecting a baby, one of the most joyous moments any couple can share, you know what her re-

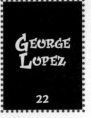

sponse was? From somewhere out near Saturn: "I need a new couch." *A new couch?* I don't think the words "Oh, my God, that's so wonderful" are in her vocabulary.

Of course, her life was no picnic. She was born in El Centro, a farming community in the Imperial Valley, 90 miles outside San Diego. She didn't know her mother. When she was seven months old, her mother was sent back to Mexico and she was given to an aunt, whose daughter was a little older. Her cousin would go to the dances and the shows. Benita was stuck at home sewing and cleaning and cooking for the entire family, a modern-day Cinderella with no hope of ever meeting Prince Charming. She admits that she was always unhappy. But for her it didn't matter how horrible it was—she'd just lick the salt off the wounds.

She ended up running away from home at sixteen. Her first husband was a Tiajuana trucker named Juan who drove back and forth across the border. He'd beat her and warn her he was going to kill her with a gun. Once Juan hit his son Johnny over the head with a shovel. Maybe that's why Uncle Johnny stutters. She lived with that husband for nineteen years, wearing her abuse as some badge of honor, somehow proud she stuck it out all that time.

"Why didn't you leave?" I asked countless times.

"Where was I going to go?" she answered every time.

A valid question when you have six kids, all torn straight from the pages of *Dysfunction Magazine.* Freddie was the oldest. For some reason they called him Al. He ended up having five kids, including a daughter who shaved her head when she was thirteen. Al was like the Team Leader of the family: the most educated, adversarial, and competitive. He married a woman who had already gone through two husbands. He ended up with a huge lump on his neck and died of cancer.

Then there were Roger and Janet. Janet hooked up with a guy named Manuel, who had this mole on the side of his nose. Part of his foot and leg had been amputated. He liked to take his frustration in life out on his wife. Yet Janet was always crying about "poor Manuel."

"Why you crying?" I'd ask her. "He's hitting you and you're crying about him?"

And let's not forget Rosemary. She had six kids of her own, a few with more than their fair share of problems, including one who got hit by a train. Don't ask. Rosemary's son Tommy was accidentally branded with an iron when he was about 18 months old. Don't ask. Today, he walks around with "Ozzy" tattooed across his knuckles. Don't ask.

And then, finally, there's John, the one who got that shovel to his head. He left the family for good about twenty years ago. Married a woman in Pittsburgh and never looked back. I've got to give John credit. He may have made the smartest move of all.

So into this mix, I arrive. The kid with the different last name. Frieda's kid. There wasn't much time left for me. I remember one time asking my grandmother if we could go to Chuck E. Cheese, my favorite neighborhood pizza place, the one with the mouse as the mascot. *"Mira, he wants to go to Chuckie Cheese. What you think I'm shitting money? You want a mouse, cabrón. Pull the refrigerator out! Pull it out! There's about five little Chuckies back there. Right there by your feet! By your FEET! Why you crying, cabrón?"*

After a lot of long, hard thought—and thousands of dollars spent on therapy analyzing this woman and my childhood—I've come to this conclusion: Without my grandmother I wouldn't have had a home; I was better off with her than I was with my mother. And without Benita, there would be no *George Lopez* show. Had my biological parents raised me, there would be no show. She doesn't realize that for all the bad stuff she put me through (and, of course, her recollection of my childhood is different from mine; she denies everything, denies all the neglect), something very good came out of it. There's this one blade of grass that grows out of the cement. How does this fucking blade make it through? That's me.

ENCANTO

Most of the men in my neighborhood were simple day laborers who waited at the same spot every day with hopes of being hired for construction. They're all gone now, guys who were forty-seven but looked like they were one hundred and seven. Dead because when they weren't laboring, they were drinking themselves to death. Every day, each with his own bottle of Hill and Hill, standing around, ragging on each other, getting fucked up, I mean *fucked* up, bonded by their love of high school football, the Dodgers, pro wrestling at Devonshire Downs (especially my hero, the magnificent Mil Máscaras), and the fact that they were all absolutely petrified of their wives.

The man I call my grandfather was named Refugio, but to family and friends he was known as Cuco. A big, strong, macho man, he dug ditches for a living, worked like a fucking mule, often doing the job of two or three men. He grew up outside Guadalajara, Mexico, was only about five-foot-eight with heavy, thick hands and a farmer's tan, yet he considered himself a bit of a dandy, always sporting a signature fedora on his head. Being a laborer, he worked only in spurts, sometimes a week or two at a time, maybe a month. He had mumps as a child, so he never had kids. Consequently, he created his own interpretations of parenthood.

"Be back in two hours," he'd tell me. "Two hours."

"Grandpa, what kid goes out on Saturday *after-noon* and has to be home by four?"

"You."

Every day, for as far back as I can remember, he used to beat into my head what it meant to be a man: "Your word is your bond" and "take responsibility." Each lesson about life strangely wrapped around his death.

"Look," he'd begin, "when I die, you're going to remember, 'cause I had these conversations with you."

I mean, I was like fucking six years old!

He loved baseball. Fridays and Saturday nights at Dodger Stadium, sitting on the benches in the left-field pavilion, a dog and soda in hand, a Mexican blanket with the deer on it over his lap to keep warm. Cheering for Garvey and Cey—El Pingüino, the Penguin. Many a time, we took our own food to the games—homemade sandwiches washed down with a huge gallon of Safeway punch. Sometimes my grandfather would open a homemade burrito and people from the next section would turn their heads. *"What the fuck is that smell? That's not popcorn. It smells like ass."*

My grandfather's other love was road trips to Mexico. We'd pack up the car and drive across the border. Man, he loved getting that tourism sticker on the windshield. He was a *turista* now, a big man from America. Bigger than he really was, barely scraping by, but people down there thought he was rich because he had a house, a wife, and a car, and talked like he had money.

Yet as confident and secure as my grandfather was in his world, if something went wrong outside that world, he caved. Wrong change in a store, no problem, *señor.* He'd been beaten down by so many obnoxious Anglo assholes in his life, his reaction was always, "I'll take another, sir." No straight-backed pride or resistance. Just the bowed head and the stooped shoulders—the national posture of millions of migrant workers who picked produce and did all the dirty work that made California the Sunshine State. One time when I was seventeen, this waiter was beyond rude to my grandparents. And I had had enough.

"Hey, man, what's your fuckin' problem?" I asked.

"Excuse me?"

"Why are you being so rude?"

My grandfather yelled at me for ten minutes. I told him the guy was being an asshole.

"But that's not your business," he said. "He works here, and it's not your business."

"Well," I replied, "if you're not going to fuckin' speak up for yourself, I am. I'm not going to let him treat you like that."

"Shhh," my grandfather said. "Someone might hear you."

And there was another side to Cuco. His major vice—like so many of his friends—was alcohol. When he drank to excess, he was a mean drunk, with an eye for confrontation. Sometimes his target was my grandmother, sometimes it was me.

I would hear them fighting when I was young, sounds no child should hear, and then he would come looking for me.

"Hide!" My grandmother yelling a word of warning, signaling my flight to the deepest, darkest corner of the nearest closet I could find. Through the crack in the door I could see his feet in front of me. Hear the curses muttered under his labored, liquored breath.

But sometimes there was no place to hide, no time to escape. Drunk, in broken English, he'd tower over me and spit out the command: "Stand right here. In front of me."

I would stand as ordered, in front of him, not moving a muscle.

"Who do you think you are?"

I didn't know what to say.

"Who do you think I am?"

Not a move. Not a word.

"Who do you think you are?"

I knew what was next. A snappy flick of his middle finger into the side of my head. A thick, fat finger that labored hard for a living tapping at my temple. It fucking hurt.

"Think." Flick! *"Who do you think you are?"* Flick! *"Who do you think I am?"* Flick!

My grandfather, who spoke mostly Spanish, and I never talked much about his life or mine. Often he was just too tired, collapsing as soon as he got home, waking up only for dinner and an hour or two of TV. I don't blame him, really; he'd accepted and dealt with the Jerry Springer Six only to discover that fate had delivered one more child. The closest we ever came to talking, really talking, was near the end. The tiles had fallen in the archway of our house, and he asked me to take him to the store for replacements. On the way over to Van Nuys, he told me for the first time what I had longed to hear my entire life.

"You're a good kid," he said. "I've raised you like my own son. Whatever happens, always remember me. Be a man. Be responsible."

I should have known he was offering up one last lesson for a reason. I should have connected the earlier angioplasty that was supposed to improve the flow of blood to his heart with the sight of him sitting on a bench not far from the house. *"I'm tired,"* he said, when I stopped to inquire. *"Too tired to walk."*

A week later, he was dead.

The scene seems surreal now, strange in ways that still ache and cut to the bone. I was just back from Fresno. My grandmother was ironing a blouse in one room; my grandfather, short of breath, clutching his chest in another.

"Let me go to the hospital," I said.

But my grandmother wouldn't hear of it. "He'll be all right, you stay here."

So I stayed and watched as he crawled into the van, hunched over, and rode away. I went to sleep. Half lazy, half awake as the phone rang a dozen times. I never got up to answer it.

The moment my grandmother walked through the door, I knew. Tears in her eyes. A blood clot in his heart.

"He's gone," she said.

How long can you carry guilt and anguish over time? For me, the answer is forever. The decision to keep my sorry, self-absorbed lazy ass in bed still haunts my heart.

I can still hear my grandmother's voice: how her husband suffered, convulsing, wetting himself in his final minutes, the horror of watching your husband die at age sixty-three.

Sitting there, listening to her, I pretty much held it together. Maybe it was shock, maybe denial. Either way, I was putting up a pretty good front, that is, until some relatives from Mexico showed up and started quizzing my grandmother on her future, looking around the house, checking out the furniture and shit.

"Get the fuck out of here," I said.

The morning of his funeral service, I was playing golf. Yeah, golf. Don't ask me why. He was at the Utter McKinley Funeral Home and I was playing eighteen holes.

When I got home, my grandmother greeted me with a request: "Can you take his clothes over to the mortuary?"

So I packed up his one sorry black suit, slim tie, and patent-leather shoes straight from south of the border and drove over to Utter McKinley's.

"You want to see him?" asked the funeral director.

No, I didn't want to see him, but somehow I knew I had to make my peace. Face the man in death whom I never quite understood in life. So I sat there alone in the room, about three rows back from the coffin. Slowly I rose, and as the man who was in essence my father came into view, I let out a sound, this loud, wailing howl, from a place I never knew existed. The funeral director busted back into the room.

"Are you all right?" he asked.

"Yeah," I lied. "I'm all right."

But I wasn't. How could I be?

I can taste the tears on my face as I think of that day, and how in

so many ways I am who I am because of him. The thing is, he never told me he loved me. Never told me he was proud. Not out loud. Never when he thought I could hear. He never knew about the day, shortly after I started doing stand-up and my publicity photos were taken, and he came home with friends one Sunday night around ten. One of my head shots lying faceup on the kitchen table, me in my room.

"Who's this?" came a voice. "Is he an actor?"

"No," said my grandfather. *"That's my grandson. He's a comedian. He's just starting out. But he's pretty good."*

The only words of praise I ever heard from him.

Thank God for tract housing. If we had been able to afford insulation, I never would have known.

I think had my grandfather lived, he would have really appreciated my climb up the ladder. When I was growing up, my grandfather would call me Encanto, which means enchanted. It's actually a good nickname, but I thought he was calling me gay or something. That's how things were: Something good was given to me, and because of my environment, I made it bad.

When I got older and my grandfather passed away, I realized how special that name was. When people ask me why I named my production company Encanto Enterprises, I smile and say it is my way of honoring a man who, in his own way, taught me what it means to be one.

THE BIKE

Whatever you wanted, it was no.

"Grandma, can I—"

"NO!"

"You don't even know what it is."

"I know your face. NO!"

Or I would want something, but they would tell me, "Mira, that's the last thing you're ever fucking going to ask for."

Sometimes they'd ask, "How old are you?"

"Nine."

"Okay, mira, think about it, because you got a long life. If you want the skates, get 'em, but that's it."

"Never mind."

"Okay, les go. Team Leader, you can't even walk, and you're going to walk with wheels, hombre. Loco. I don't have time to teach you. Either you know, or you know."

You know, other parents would buy their kid a bike and it would already come assembled—helmet waiting on the handlebars. "JOSH, that's YOURS!"

"Do you really MEAN it, Father?"

In my house? My grandfather's half drunk on Christmas dragging the box in the living room . . . "Hey, mira, that's the bike you wanted. Why you crying? Those better be tears of joy, *cabrón;* I had to pull the fucking bike all the way from the garage. It say, Huffy, yeah, I'm huffy right now. I can berly get air. They must know how far you had to pull it. Huffy. *Mira,* we're going to put it together, right now, I'm feeling good . . . I drank at work and I came home . . . I'm already, *cómo se dice* . . . light-headed."

So my grandfather finally puts the bike together . . . and there're parts left over. Big ones.

"Get on."

"Get on? But there are still parts."

"Get, *mira, cabrón,* get on, and we'll see what happens; if it runs good. A lot of times they send extra parts. As a . . . pre-cautionary measure, *mira.*"

"Where're the training wheels?"

"*Cabrón,* how old are you—four? You don't need training wheels. When I was your age I was already driving the fucking car. Over the Grapevine . . . carrying grapes from Fresno . . . Four years old, you can't ride a bike. I'll teach you . . . like that.

"*Mira,* get on. Your feet don't touch the pedals? *Mira,* the way I teach you, they don't need to. The pedal comes up, push it back down. When it comes up, push it down. Push it down. Don't let it hit you in the back of the leg—it'll cut you. You don't even need both legs—just one. Here, let me hold the handlebars . . . Go to the car and wait for me. Ready? On three. One, two—

"Push the pedal down! Push IT DOWN! THE PEDAL—

"He fell on the grass, he's all right.

"You crying? You want to go to McDonald's? A Happy Meal? Well, then, get happy, *cabrón.*"

ME AND ERNIE AND FREDDIE

I grew up on a cul-de-sac—French for dead end—between a Laundromat and the I-5 Freeway in a cramped, dim low-lying home on Hager Street in the Mission Hills section of San Fernando. My grandparents had moved around quite a bit before settling on Hager in the early sixties, and forty years later my grandmother still lives in the same old place.

It's the kind of neighborhood where most of the houses haven't changed all that much, nobody moves too far away, trucks get parked at odd angles in driveways, and high school girls have a way of getting pregnant.

It was such a sad little block not even the ice cream man would bother driving down my street. There I'd be, like a little trouper, waiting at the curb, hearing those little jingle bells, and he'd hang a U-turn and cruise away. I'd have to chase him for three blocks before he'd stop.

Yes, our little corner of the Valley could have been named Without Hope. In the early sixties, Mexicans weren't even a class of people in Southern California. Millions had risked life and limb to come across the border with little more than the *camisas* on their backs, chasing the American Dream or some small portion of it with little or no success—especially on Hager. Nobody amounted to much of anything where I lived. High school graduation was a pipe dream. No-

body worked with their head. Nobody saved. Nobody stood up for themselves.

These days, late at night, I'll sometimes drive those streets and think back to the ten-to-fifteen-block area between San Fernando Mission, Laurel Canyon, and Brand Boulevard, where me and my friends all lived, guys like Ernie, Arnold, Andy, Russell, and 'Memo. I was the only one who lived on Hager. The rest of our crowd resided just a few short blocks away on Mott, Macneil, or Maclay. I can play back in my head countless games of football and baseball in the streets, swims at Paxton Park, and our daily ventures to the Little Red Drug Store for candy, Bob's Records for posters, and People's for jeans.

My best friend growing up was Ernie Arellano. We met in the sandbox at San Fernando Preschool. We hit it off right away. We were both misfits, kinda like the kids in the movie *The Sandlot,* only with concrete instead of sand. We were also pretty shy, and that's how we bonded. It was a ten-minute walk down a tight alley and under the freeway to get from my house to Ernie's. He lived across the street from Thrifty, home to our first official strip mall. The mall has seen better days. Family Fashion, First Bargain, and the Lavendería are all still there. The Kmart is now called Ken Mart.

I was the only Mexican child in my neighborhood (maybe in the country) with no siblings. All my friends had brothers and sisters. Except me. Ernie was as close as I got to having a brother.

Growing up, it was always George and Ernie. Not Ernie and George, but George and Ernie. Me and Ernie. If I said that once, I said it a thousand times growing up. Me and my friend Ernie are going out to play. Me and Ernie are going to the store. Me and Ernie got this thing going with the ladies, man. He had a nuclear family; I had a *telenovela.* Either way, we did everything together. Riding bikes, walking to school, parties—we did it all.

Me and Ernie . . .

OTHER VOICES—ERNIE ARELLANO

I never knew George's father, and my memory of his mother is vague. His grandmother reminded me of Yvonne DeCarlo. Not Lily Munster, the character DeCarlo played, but of Yvonne DeCarlo the actress. And his grandfather reminded me of Richard Deacon from the old Dick Van Dyke Show.

One of my earliest memories of George is of the two of us walking home from school. We were in first grade, probably about five years old. When we got to my aunt and uncles' house, where I'd stay until my parents picked me up on their way home from work, I said to George, "See you tomorrow," and George started to cry. My uncle came out and asked George what was wrong, and George said, "I forgot where I live." So we all got in my uncle's car, and George was like, "Take a right, and another right, now a left, and it's the second house." George knew exactly where he lived, he just didn't want to walk home alone.

The kid from *Home Alone* had nothing on me.

I didn't know there was a name for children like me until one day I saw a commercial about a latchkey kid letting himself into an empty house after school. Every day, around three, that was me, letting myself in the kitchen door or slipping through an open window.

When you're home alone you find love in other forms and faces. Some kids talk to their toys. Some make up imaginary friends. Others live in imaginary worlds populated with people who don't argue or drink, folks who think nothing of giving you a hug or a kiss or a compliment or a smile. The people I interacted with on those lonely afternoons lived in a box. My electronic family—variety show hosts like Mike Douglas, Merv Griffin, and Dinah Shore—were always

inviting funny and interesting people over to their place. Jimmie "JJ" Walker, Richard Pryor, and George Carlin were some of my early favorites, guys me and Ernie would sprint home from school to see.

Consequently, we got the comedy bug young, and we knew all the comics—the famous and the not so famous. One day we were cruising Laurel Canyon Boulevard in North Hollywood, and we passed this car going in the other direction. We both shouted, "That's Johnny Dark!" You have to really know your comics to remember—much less to have recognized—Johnny Dark, but he was a fixture at the Comedy Store in the late seventies with the likes of David Letterman, Elayne Boosler, Jay Leno, Steve Landesberg, and Pryor. We whipped a U-turn in the middle of Laurel Canyon and followed Johnny Dark all the way home. I jumped out and approached him in his driveway. "I am George Lopez," I said, "and I want to be a comedian, too." He told us to wait outside, went in his house, came back with two eight-by-tens, autographed one for each of us, and just hung out and talked shop. He was so cool, and it was cool to be in the presence of a professional comedian.

It was in that electronic box in the summer of 1974 that I met my new best friend. Over time he would become my guardian angel, the one who watched over my career from above. And today, in the strangest of ways, I have become the keeper of his flame.

I was all of thirteen when the promotion came on, a classic sixty-four Chevy with pom-poms and the antenna and the little dog in the back window followed by the words "Coming this fall." From then on I'd sit in front of the TV, watching it like a hawk, waiting, hoping just to see the promo again, to see the kid, this Chico with the bedroom eyes, who wore denim like we did, cool as shit with that droopy mustache, long hair, and lover-boy body.

My idol . . . Freddie Prinze.

Think Robin Williams in the eighties or Chris Rock today, and that was Freddie Prinze Sr. in the early 1970s. Words like "creative genius" get tossed around a lot in my business, but they're actually on target when it comes to the comedic talents of one Frederick Karl Pruetzel, born June 22, 1954, to a Puerto Rican mother and E. Karl Pruetzel, the Hungarian taskmaster Freddie never really liked.

He grew up up in Washington Heights, New York—"a slum with trees," he called it—studied music and karate, and dreamed of fame and fortune. His idol was Lenny Bruce. Eventually Freddie got his break earning stand-up shots at New York landmarks like the Improv and Catch a Rising Star, mesmerizing people with his comedic and imitative talents. Before long he got the call every comedian died for back then—a guest spot on *The Tonight Show* starring Johnny Carson. Freddie laid Johnny out that night, so much so that he was offered a coveted seat on Carson's couch. That contributed to his meteoric rise and led to an audition in the summer of 1974 that would change—and eventually help end—his life.

OTHER VOICES—RON DE BLASIO, FREDDIE PRINZE'S MANAGER

> *I am on the road with Pryor and we're going to Chicago and we finish a show and Richie says, "C'mon, we're going to a club tonight."*
>
> *I say, "I'm not going to a club."*
>
> *He says, "No, you're going to come to a club. We're going to Mr. Kelly's to see this guy, a friend of mine, a comic."*
>
> *I say, "Who's this guy?"*
>
> *He says, "Motherfucker, just c'mon."*
>
> *"What's he like?"*
>
> *"He's Spanish, sort of, from New York—he's like me."*
>
> *"He's like you?"*
>
> *"Yeah."*
>
> *"Hmmm."*

So we walk into Mr. Kelly's, and I know the club pretty well. Bette Midler broke out there. Streisand played there. Mr. Kelly's was one of those places you had to play.

So I see Freddie and he's funny. His language is a little salty for a nineteen-year-old kid, but the jazz people like him—it's an old crowd, old Chicago patrons, drinking, couples, some not with their wives, Frank's Chicago. So I sorta liked him, and we go outside, and Freddie says to me, "So, you saw my act, would you consider representing me?"

Without batting an eye I say, "Represent you? I don't even know if I like you." And that was the end of that.

Then the show gets on the air and he's out here. I pick up a copy of Time *magazine and the title of the article is "The Prinze of Prime Time."*

So I start to ask around about Freddie, and hear there're lots of problems, the least of which is his manager. Freddie calls me up once more and we chat, but again nothing really comes of it. Then one night, late at night, Freddie says, "Listen, I have an attorney, David Braun. Do you know him?"

I say, "Yeah, good guy, straight shooter."

"Listen, I've worked it out whereby for the length of the contract I have with my manager I will pay him what I have to pay him, so I have to have a reduced commission on what I pay you. But just as soon as that obligation is over, I'll pay your full management commission."

"Okay," I say, "sounds fine."

Freddie Prinze was the thing that really brought me and Ernie together. We had both seen Freddie perform on the *Midnight Special.* He was wearing bell-bottom jeans and a rhinestone shirt, and me and Ernie were both bitten. Up to that point, the only Latino on TV we

could relate to was Pepino on *The Real McCoys.*
Freddie Prinze was our Beatles, and that show was
our *Ed Sullivan Show.*

To me, Freddie was the second-generation Desi
Arnaz. Desi was the brains behind *I Love Lucy,* the
man Bob Hope once described as one of the smartest
people he'd met in Hollywood. Desi invented the three-camera format that sitcoms still use today, but because of the language barrier—
not to mention the *color* barrier—never got the recognition he
deserved.

Given Hollywood history, it's no surprise that the star of *Chico
and the Man* wasn't Freddie but rather veteran Oscar-winning actor
Jack Albertson, who played Ed Brown. A crotchety old man, Ed was
the cantankerous owner of an auto garage in a run-down—or over-
run, in Ed's mind—East LA barrio. Freddie played this wisecracking
Chicano named Chico Rodriguez, Ed's eventual partner in the
garage.

At least that was the premise on paper. No different from a hundred other oil-and-water sitcoms. Except in this case you had James
Komack as the executive producer and an actor like Albertson who
was willing to share the stage with a comet like Freddie that streaks
across the sky once every decade or so.

The show premiered on September 13, 1974. The first words I
heard were, *"Chico . . . don't be discouraged . . . the man he ain't so hard
to understand,"* written and sung by the incomparable José ("Light My
Fire") Feliciano. In the very first scene, a rumpled Albertson is mum-
bling and grumbling his way down the stairs from his room above the
garage. He kicks a water can out of the way for good measure. The
world was changing, and Ed Brown wanted nothing to do with it.
He shuffles over to the cash register where, it turns out, he keeps a
glass stashed and pours himself an eye-opener before delivering his
first shot of the show: "In those days Mexicans knew their place—
Mexico."

Watching that first episode today I can still see what lured me in,
what lured America in. From the very first time Freddie literally rode

into Ed's life on the back of his bicycle and said, "Oh, *buenos días,*" Freddie sizzled and smoked and proved the perfect foil for Albertson.

"I won a Silver Star in Vietnam," Chico says.

"Where?" counters Brown. "In a crap game?"

"I want my place in the sun," says Chico.

"Then go to the beach."

They stayed that way for much of the next three years, most of the time on Friday nights between eight-thirty and nine. To a thirteen-year-old it was a "good" show; to an adult, Komack & Co. offered a lighthearted but pointed look at family and cultural and social issues of the time. Like the time a young Spanish-speaking pregnant girl arrives at the garage, and Ed assumes that Chico is the father, or the time Ed gets the wrong idea about what Chico and his girlfriend were doing in the back of his van; or in another, for pure laughs, Ed becomes convinced he's lost his touch as a mechanic.

With a supporting cast that included Scatman Crothers, Della Reese, and Charo, and guest stars like Shelley Winters, Sammy Davis Jr., and Jim Backus, the show was a smash from the start, rising all the way to number one in the ratings. Over time, the opening credit sequence slicked up a bit—the shots of the LA barrio became hipper—and so did the billing. What was once "Introducing Freddie Prinze" soon changed to "Also Starring."

As year one turned into two and three, Chico moves in with Ed, and Ed falls in love with Chico's aunt Connie. At the same time, Americans fell in love with Freddie. No one more so than me. One day I sat down and wrote a letter to NBC asking, in my best penmanship, to please, please, send me two tickets to a studio taping in Burbank of *Chico and the Man.* Sure enough, a couple of weeks later an enveloped arrived addressed to me. Inside, a letter and two tickets to the show. It was like winning Lotto.

"I want to go," I told my grandmother. "Please take me."

She said nothing, so I counted the days until, finally, it was time. I still see her in the kitchen and me asking, pleading, begging her to take me. And her turning and saying, "I'm not going to take you. We're not going anywhere."

There's crying, and then there are tears that tear a thirteen-year-old's heart out. I lost a piece of mine in the kitchen that day.

Yet, in a strange way, from a distance I drew even closer to Freddie as he skyrocketed to fame, and phrases like "Loooking Goood" and "Ees not my job" exploded into pop culture: Freddie jetting to Vegas for sold-out stand-up gigs, recording a comedy album, major guest shots on everything from *Dean Martin Comedy Roasts* to the inaugural ball for President Jimmy Carter in Washington, DC. Overnight, comedic fame and fortune mixed with another combustible fuel: major heartthrob status for the *Tiger Beat* and *Sixteen* crowd and the intoxicating scent of cover stories in both *Rolling Stone* and *Playboy*.

It was while on vacation that Freddie met the woman who, for a while, would help him handle celebrity, the increasing tug-of-war for his time and talent. He and Katherine Cochran were married in August 1975 and later had a child, Freddie James Prinze, in March of 1976. By then, it turns out, Freddie was drowning bit by bit, his marriage faltering, his mind altered by drugs and distracted by a breach-of-contract lawsuit by a former manager.

I knew everything there was to know about him. Fuck, I *was* Freddie.

His picture hung on my bedroom wall. Day after day I stared at it, thinking, *I can be a comic. I can do what Freddie is doing. I want to make people laugh.*

OTHER VOICES—RON DE BLASIO

So we started working together and became pretty tight. Went through all the machinations with him. He had a drug problem, but it never really showed in TV. I knew that he didn't like drugs; it was just an escape. He was an insecure kid. We used to talk an awful lot about his problem, and I tried to assure him I understood where he was. Twenty-year-old kid, people asking you to entertain adults, to hold their attention with things that are relatable to them, and you're from the streets, and they already have you pegged as a TV person, so they expect this nice little kid, not motherfucker this, motherfucker that. No one expected the racial jokes, the sex jokes.

It's the next-to-the-last day of shooting for the season, and he called me up a couple of times that day. He was down, depressed, not all that unusual. Kathy and he not getting along; the attorneys were saying bad things. And I said that's just posturing. He was upset about the divorce.

That night, he called again. He said, "You know, Ron, I feel badly. I don't feel good." What is this all about? "I'm being harassed. Tomorrow is our last day of shooting."

I said, "Look, look where you are now. You're so far ahead of everybody else. Tomorrow is the last day of the show. After that you're going to have your own special with NBC. We're going to produce another TV sitcom. We'll get through the summer. It will be fine. You'll get through it."

He said, "Okay, fine, okay, I've got it. Thanks, thanks, Ron. I got it."

About ten minutes later his assistant, Carol Novak, phoned. She said everything was fine, whatever it was I said, worked. He just shot right up. She said everything was good, so much so that she could leave. That he was going to get ready to go to work the next day.

I asked her what happened on the set, and she said he had done some quaaludes. I said, "Okay. How many?"

She said, "I don't know. I asked him and he said he had taken . . . seven."

So he took those quaaludes that day, didn't eat anything, so

he was down. But by the time I spoke to him, he was up, and I thought, okay he's coming out of it, he's going to be okay. *So that was the end of it. I went to bed.*

The phone rings at three o'clock in the morning. My wife says, "I don't think this call is going to be a good one."

Dusty, his business manager, is on the phone. He's sobbing, out of breath, as if he'd run a marathon. He couldn't catch his breath. He said, "He did it, Ron. He did it."

"Did what?"

"He did it. He said he would and he did it."

"Okay Dusty, just chill out, what did he do? What did he do? What's happened?" .

He said Freddie shot himself.

When I got to the hospital, it was pretty apparent this kid was gone. On life support. Just a mess. Freddie's attorney David Braun and I moved to a corner down the hall, each giving counsel and comfort to one another—David giving me a lot of comfort. It was then I walked up to Freddie's mother, father, and Kathy. With very few words, we all came to the same conclusion, but all of us wanted to go in and see Freddie one last time. We did. He was resting and looking at peace. We said goodbye.

In January 1977 I was in the tenth grade at San Fernando High. Every morning this old white RCA clock-radio woke me up. It wasn't much, plastic and about the size of a brick, beaten and battered like so many things in my life. But unlike my mother or uncles, it was reliable. The sounds of KHJ 93 every weekday at five-fifty A.M. announced it was essentially time to drag my ass out of bed and shuffle over to San Fernando High.

Invariably I was greeted by conflicting reports—sunny weather,

shitty traffic. But not January 28, 1977. That day the announcer's words seemed to travel through a mist. What was he saying? Comedian Freddie Prinze had *what?* Was *where?* In the hospital. *Self-inflicted wounds?*

I sat on the edge of my bed with my mouth open for about twenty minutes. Just in shock.

At school, it was all anyone talked about. It was a Friday.

I cried. My hero, my caregiver, the man who pulled me through the huge layer of sadness that was my life had shot himself? Shit. Shit. Shit.

The next day Freddie was dead at the age of twenty-two.

When Freddie died, for me and Ernie it was like when John Lennon was shot. A year after he died, me and Ernie made a pilgrimage to the Comstock Hotel, where Freddie committed suicide. We went upstairs and stood outside Room 216. We didn't talk. We just shook our heads.

Did some of me die with him? You bet it did. It was like learning that an older brother had committed suicide, losing my best friend in life when I needed him most. How to mourn? What to do?

The papers said something about a service—couldn't very well attend that—adding that Freddie would be buried at Forest Lawn Memorial-Park in the Hollywood Hills. Little did I know at the time, but Forest Lawn is the Ritz-Carlton of resting places—five-star living for the dead. (Pretty much the only Mexicans "resting" in Forest Lawn are the ancient Aztec artifacts in the fascinating Plaza of Mexican Heritage up in the back . . . or on their lunch break.) Bette Davis is buried at Forest Lawn; so is George Raft. It is an elegant, pastoral place—more than 350 magnificent acres overlooking the back lot of Warner Bros. Studios. There are no fences, and families are advised that only fresh flowers are allowed and that "nonconforming" decorations such as borders, planter boxes, ornaments, statues, or glass are not permitted and will be removed.

I had no idea how to find Freddie. But I knew we needed to talk. I figured, shit, how hard can it be, until I got there and saw those 350 acres spread out over seemingly endless arching hills. All I knew was he wasn't buried in the ground, and there had to be a lot of flowers, so off I went in my seventy-six gray LTD, big monster car, more primer than paint, searching for massive bouquets of fresh-cut arrangements, up and around and around and over and around until finally, way back in the upper reaches of the place, I get out at something called the Courts of Remembrance. Silently it screamed marble and money, the kind of spot old Hollywood would hang out, so I wandered around, glancing around and down the paths, still not sure, until, in the Sanctuary of Light, a garden of flowers caught my eye. *Freddie,* I thought. And I was right. Far right, two up, two in, was his crypt.

•••

Freddie Prinze
We Love You
23rd Psalm
1954–1977

•••

Father Karl is interred on Freddie's left. To the right rests tough guy Raft. But all I saw was Freddie, and I did what I still do today—started crying. After a while I found myself leaning forward to touch the plaque for strength, feeling it shift slightly in my hand.

Mmmm. Kinda loose here.

It felt like, well, the kind of plate if you were of a mind and wiggled it back and forth and around a bit, then a bit more, then, looking around, a little harder, it might just . . . pop off into your hand.

Now, before you call the cops, put the phone down. Kathy Prinze, Freddie's widow, knows I have the marker. As with many things involving Freddie and me, the path to her finding out is a bit otherworldly but worth the trip.

It starts out with us wanting to buy a house in Toluca Lake, me coming home from a trip and Ann saying, "Guess who we're meeting at two?"

"Who?"

"Kathy Prinze."

"What?"

"The woman who was with Freddie the night he died, Carol Novak, his personal assistant and Kathy's friend, is our Realtor."

"I'm not going to go."

"You GOT to go."

"No, I'm NOT going to go."

"Not only are you GOING TO GO, you're going to tell Kathy how you feel about Freddie."

So off we go, and I'm standing there in front of Freddie's wife, a vision to me, just standing, in the midst of a long, uncomfortable pause, when Ann chimes in, "Kathy, George was a huge fan of Freddie."

So I tell Kathy how much and for how long I loved her husband. Where I am because of him. What drove me out of my house, off my street, into comedy was him. Kathy begins to cry, I begin to cry, Ann begins to cry.

Eventually, we all become quite close. So close that not long ago, Kathy gave me the gift of a small leather key ring.

"It was Freddie's," she said.

Each time I step on the set I slide that key ring into the right pocket of my pants. It's my good luck charm, my way of keeping Freddie's spirit at my side. My way of saying, *"Gracias, ese,* look around, this is your success too."

So one day, given all that Kathy has meant to us, Ann finds it in her heart to inform Kathy that I have the plaque.

"You know what?" Kathy said after a moment. "I always wondered what happened. But of all the people who could have taken it, I'm glad it was George."

For some reason, while the drug-induced deaths of Lenny Bruce, Jim Morrison, Jimi Hendrix, and Janis Joplin only increased their popularity, with Freddie, for whatever reason, it was just the opposite with his suicide. His long shadow only shortened.

I've always believed we should remember the way Freddie *lived*—not the way he died. So it was the first week in March 2004 that I proudly took the stage at the Hollywood Palladium to present a TV Land Award honoring, for the first time, the life and legacy of Freddie Prinze Sr., before a crowd packed  with my childhood heroes—Tony Orlando and Dawn, Patty Duke, and stars from *The Beverly Hillbillies*, *The Munsters*, *Love Boat*, and *Gilligan's Island*.

I felt something like Tom Hanks in the movie *Cast Away*, lost on a desert island, then, finally, after thirty years, getting to say "Here's your package" to Freddie. Here it is, man, after all the bullshit you went through from the Mexican community because you were Puerto Rican, because you took your own life, here's your award, presented by a forty-plus-year-old Mexican dude who idolized your every word, the full-grown seed of what you and you alone planted in 1974.

Feeling the love, I took a chance and slipped into a dead-on impression of my man Chico. The audience ate it up. I loved Freddie then, I said, and I love him now. Don't ever forget Freddie, I said. Remember the way he lived, not the way he died.

And then I called his only son to the stage.

Yes, it was that kind of moment. The first time the actor Freddie Prinze Jr. had decided to recognize his father in such a public way.

We stood there together, seemingly alone, and then Freddie hugged me—a long, deep hug that seemed to travel through time, connecting two young sons who never knew their dads, yet mysteriously drawn, over the years, to the same man, and now sharing his night as one. "Stay here with me," Freddie whispered. So I did. Beaming with pride as he accepted the award, truly felt the greatness of his father, I think, for the first time.

And mark this down: Very soon this *Home Alone* kid is going to buy a big, big house overlooking Los Angeles. And when I do, I plan on putting a bench in the backyard and giving Freddie's marker a proper resting place—a breathtaking view of the stars for a star, a comedic comet, who did nothing less than change my life.

Ernie and I eventually split up in the early nineties over some stupid money shit. We spent years apart with no attempts to reconcile. Both of us could easily have found the other but never did. One time he came to The Ice House to see me and all he said was, "That was a good crowd." Nothing about the real issues that separated us. I didn't know what to do.

There is a transportation guy named Irv who works on the show. Turns out Ernie's sister, Dorie, works for Irv's wife's dentist, and through them, I got Ernie's mother's number. Thanks to my therapist I've begun to close circles in my life, and Ernie was one of the biggest. Today, Ernie is an assistant superintendent for a division of the second-largest home builder in the country. He never married, but in 1987 he had a son, my godson, Neil. Neil has turned out to be a promising amateur boxer with aspirations of fighting in the Olympics someday.

About a year ago, Ernie was driving home from a job in West Covina when his cell phone rang. I said hello. It had been over a decade since we'd spoken, and he was shocked to hear my voice, though he knew it was me right away. I said, "I want to get together," and Ernie said, "Why?" I told him, "I am in therapy, and your name comes up a lot." He apologized. I told him that I never stopped being his friend. I invited Ernie and Neil to one of my shows last October at the Universal Amphitheatre.

Toward the end of the show I looked out on the sell-out crowd of some 6,500 people, and I shared with the audience my story about working at ITT in Van Nuys and coming to the amphitheater with my friend Ernie to see Comic Relief, and how we wanted to jump the fence because we didn't have tickets and couldn't get in. But I'll tell you what, sixteen years later and comin' through the front door is a lot better than jumpin' over that fuckin' fence . . .

I wouldn't have stood on that stage or be where I am today

without a lot of comic *belief,* and nobody helped or
believed more than my friend Ernie.

OTHER VOICES—ERNIE ARELLANO

*Even though I am very distant from it, I am very proud. George
and I were like Sears Roebuck, and I am Roebuck. Who knows
Roebuck, right? But I am proud to have been a part of it from the
start.*

*I know it sounds bad, but sometimes I wish George had not
become successful—not because I am jealous but because I miss the
way things used to be. I miss the days when we would go to As-
troburger on Santa Monica after his shows and just sit and recap
the act.*

BACKYARD WEDDINGS

Almost anything interesting in a Chicano family either begins or ends in the backyard.

One big reason is that we drink more than anyone else. No one teaches us how to drink.

Other people can have a social glass of wine.

"Would you like another Chardonnay, Frank?"

"Oh, I better not, I'm starting to get a little tipsy."

Chicanos? We wake up tipsy. How many times have you woken up still drunk? "Cabrón, I'm not going to eat 'cause I'm still buzzing."

My uncle Victor used to drink everything. Champagne, beer, tequila, schnapps, sloe gin, Listerine, Scope, whatever you had. And it was funny.

For about three minutes.

"Victor, do you dance?" And the rest of the night, there he'd be, slow dancing by himself in the backyard, and later when you tried to pry the car keys out of his hand, he just kept saying, "I'm all right. I'm all right. Mira, I don't need no designated *como se llama*. I drive better when I'm drunk." Then he proceeds to start the car—twice.

More than once Uncle Victor put on a tremendous display of drunken revelry at a backyard wedding or birthday party. But weddings were the best.

You don't go to the Hilton and rent the California—"Are

you here for the O'Brien wedding in the California Room? Can you sign the guest book? Fantastic."

My grandma would be like, "'Tás loco, California Room, mira, the backyard, it's California también. We'll open the garage and put the DJ in there."

Then, of course, in the morning they'd bring the bride out to the "reception area."

"Qué pasó? What's wrong with you?"

"I don't like my wedding in the backyard."

"Oh, mira, you don't want the wed-ding in the backyard . . . well, tell the Team Leader to get some money."

"But I don't want my wedding in the backyard."

"Listen, let me tell you: I lived a long life. I been to Mexico . . . and Las Vegas. One time I went to Fresno, pero, but just on the bus. I been around. And tonight the backyard is not going to look like it looks now. Bonito. Mira, we're going to move all the cars out. Even that one—Rudy's going to get a truck from work and we're going to drag it out. And we're going to cut the grass—nice. And the driveway . . . we're going to put sand on the oil, and it's going to be the dance floor. And on the clothesline, mira, we're going to put a sheet . . . the VIP area. The rest of the house . . . is going to be general admission."

And there's never an open bar—they don't trust us enough. You go to a wedding where there're Anglos and there's a guy standing there in a tuxedo shirt with a tie—"Hi, apple martini, oh, fantastic." Us? "Hey, where'd you get that beer?" Shhhhh. "On the side of the garage, I've got a twelve-pack. Don't tell nobody, don't tell nobody, man. It's your wedding, eh, if it wasn't, you'd have to get your own beer."

And the hard liquor? Put away. Crown Royal . . . "Mira, Crown Royal, he's got a job now"—but they tell only selected people. "Hey, psst, hey, you want Crown Royal? Go to the baby's room. And under his head, pero, take a little and put it back. And turn the birds so they sing again, mira, turn . . ."

MI TÍA

My aunts were never sexual people.

Mis tías were all short and they were kinda gorditas. They all had, like, six kids, and they were never sexual. You know, now some mothers, they're attractive. Mis tías, they would have slippers on about three in the afternoon. They would walk out of the house in slippers. But when they ate ribs they turned into some screen siren, eating in the backyard, smacking their lips—"Give me more sauce, porque quiero más"—and one of my uncles would be at the end of the bench all pissed off.

"How come you don't suck me like that? I can never get NOTHING!"

And mi tía would never even miss a beat: "You know why, cabrón, porque this bone is hard."

Having said that, many Chicanos have a tía who, when she was young, was fine. And the only pictures in the house now are when she was fine. "Mira, don't take a picture of me, porque my—I don't have a tooth right here, mira." But when she was young, beautiful, that's all she ever talks about.

"Mira, when I was young, chichis, mira, look. And my nipples would be out. I used to go to the bakery, they would give me bread, hombre. I would lean down. 'Give me those.' And the man would just keep putting them in the bag."

But now she's old, about seventy-two, with dyed hair, platinum blonde. I have an aunt who's darker than me with platinum blonde hair. She looks like a negative from the pictures. "Ah, cabrón, we don't have to show her the picture, we just show her the negative."

And she thinks everyone's jealous. "Mira, look, everybody looking at me, hombre." With the leather miniskirt, the halter top, the pumps with the glass heels, seventy-two years old. And the second toe—the one with the toe ring—is longer than the big toe. And when she walks by the ring scrapes the cement—ay, ay, ay, ay, ay.

And she gets so drunk that when she goes to the bathroom, she comes back with her dress tucked up in her panty hose. Her thong isn't even in her crack—it's off to the side.

"Don't tell her. Don't tell her."

"Look, everybody's looking at me."

"Don't tell her."

"Hombre, cabrón, I'll dance all night long. Mira, vámonos. Watcha."

So naturally we just encourage her. "Alle, Tía, alle!" And my grandmother will say, "Put that thong in the middle, cochina!"

"No, mamá, mira. Because it hurts like that, ay. It feels like it's tearing me in half. Like that, I can't dance."

Now she begins the dance like someone straight out of Boogie Nights, waving her arms, swaying to the música.

"I got to be free like this, freelance, mira, I'm your puppet. Mira, I'm your puppet, watch out . . .

FIRST TIMES

*"**I** know at times I can't make it but eventually I will. And I will hit the American people like a hammer. I will be the best."*

I wrote those words on a single slip of white paper, long faded, now framed, on August 6, 1979, shortly after graduating from San Fernando Valley High School.

Of course, given an unfortunate set of circumstances that seemed to stalk my life during this period, I didn't actually *graduate* with the rest of my class. I did get to don the cap and gown, though, strolling across stage with my friend Andy to collect a box missing a diploma. That would have to wait until I made up that illusive English class over the summer. Parading in front of my long-lost mom, shocked that she'd showed up, along with her ancient husband, *Senior Citizen*. Mom was a real peach—no camera, and just the picture of attitude: *"Oh, look at him. Mr. Oh You Think You're All Bad. Mr. High School Diploma. Mr. I Know Where Africa Is."* My grandfather, who had been on me for years to do well in school, chose to stay at home. To this day I don't know why. But I didn't care. Even though I had just scraped by, I was the first member of my very extended family to graduate from high school, and I was damn proud of it. *That's right, Chandler, the brown man with the big head said* high *school.*

In fact, I remember the period between eight and eighteen as full of firsts—first kiss, first job, first stand-up . . .

. . . first goat kill.

That precious moment arrived when I was all of about thirteen, and my little buddy got eliminated—where else but in the backyard. There we were playing that day—*"Vámonos, c'mon, Chivo. Come on, Chivo. Jump! Jump! Chivo!"*—when my grandmother starts yelling from the porch, "I told you not to play with the food, *cabrón*. What are you doing?"

"I'm playing with . . . with . . . what should I call him?"

"How about Temporary? *Porque* he is going in the hole, *cabrón*, in about five minutes."

Five years earlier I'd been part of another first—my first trip to the plate thanks to that glorified form of Chicano Day Care known as Little League.

"Mira, put him in the Little League, and we'll go to Las Vegas on Saturday."

We'd have practice and our games in luscious San Fernando Park on Rock Field, so named for the impressive stone stands and bathrooms. I loved baseball and being part of a team for the first time in my life.

To this day I'm a team guy. While some TV stars see their weekly shows in a one-way mirror and rarely mix with the cast and crew, I'm different. I'm more like two-time Super Bowl MVP Tom Brady—in the middle of things yet focused on bringing out the best in my teammates. That's the lesson I learned in Little League.

Perhaps my grandfather would have learned that lesson too, but the man who made all those trips to Dodger Stadium, for some reason hated watching his grandson play.

"Well, you're gonna lose," he said. "What am I going to go for—to see you lose?"

"But, Cuco . . ."

"What happened last time?"

"We . . . lost."

"Well . . . ? "

He did, however, come twice. Surprised the shit out of me. The last time I heard him before I saw him, rolling up along the left field line in his beat-up old Bonneville, polishing off, I'm sure, what was left of that six-pack of beer riding shotgun.

As fate would have it, I hit my only home run that night. I was trotting around second and headed for third when I looked into the outfield and saw my grandfather positioned at a bush beyond the left field fence . . . taking a leak.

"Hey," he yelled, turning around. "How come you're running so slow? They get you out?"

No, Grandpa. But if you see a hole I could crawl in, that would be great.

Then there was a Chicano family favorite—the ever-popular First Arrest.

Mine came courtesy of my cousin Bob and a bag of marijuana, just as I was nearing the end of ninth grade at San Fernando Junior High. Weed I accepted if for no other reason than being raised in a culture where people seem incapable of uttering the simplest word in Spanish or English.

No.

Why? Cue the Chicano choir: Because like so many of you I was afraid *People Were Not Going To Like Me.*

So Bob handed me the pot. "You get high, right?" he said.

Not really. But not knowing what to say or do, I took it. And since bringing it home for my grandmother to find was *not* an option, I took it to school.

Meanwhile, these other *bueys*—funny but dumb—had cracked into the school cafeteria and swiped a numbered roll of lunch tickets,

handing them out around school like they were for-ties. Naturally, I take the tickets too—can't say no—and put them in my wallet, which seems logical until the principal decides to play Columbo and search every locker. I'm in gym class at the time suffering further humiliation in the form of a tight white T-shirt and shorts, when suddenly I hear an announcement: *"George Lopez, please report to the gym office. Mr. Lopez, to the gym office."* Shit.

Sure enough, I get dressed, then arrested and hauled away to the local police station conveniently located right across the street. No handcuffs, just a classic junior high perp walk designed to show every last teenager the perils of drug use. Suddenly I'm the talk of the town. Mr. Kingpin. Mr. Drug Dealer. Mr. Mug Shot. Mr. Fingerprints. Mr. One Phone Call.

"Mrs. Gutierrez?"

"Yes."

"This is Officer Lilos from the San Fernando Police Depart-ment."

"Yes."

"We have your grandson down here."

I can hear her on the phone. "It can't be my George."

"Yes. Mrs. Gutierrez, we have George Lopez for possession of marijuana. Could you come down and get him."

Well, she came down and got me, all right, right after I sang like a fucking canary. Came right down and took me home, then sent me to my Uncle Freddie in Chula Vista, near San Diego, for a month. The change in venue designed to alter my behavior. Probably also to save my life. Had my grandfather found out, he would have killed me.

But it wasn't like I was messed up or anything; hell, by ninth grade I had barely kissed a girl—Eva Lopez, sixth grade, closed-lips, being the first—and had downed maybe one or two wine coolers my entire life. To me, happiness was still playing in the street with Ernie, Arnold, and Guillermo, cruising over to Bob's Records or JC Penney.

So there I was, all of about fifteen, dark skinned and insecure, but when I walked into San Fernando High in the fall of 1976, into this sea of brown and black and white faces, I had an identity: Thanks to getting whacked for the weed, I registered on the radar screen. People knew me.

Sometimes at night, after dropping off my grandmother at the house on Hager, I'll drive around San Fernando High. Back then it was more like *Fast Times at Ridgemont High* . . . only for Chicano stoners. Today, times haven't changed all that much. Yeah, there's a lot of new construction going on, but for the most part it is now what it was then—a big, rambling riot of low-lying brick buildings spread out over an entire city block. I can look around the quad and almost see Ernie and me sitting on the picnic tables, hanging out.

I wasn't in Cool Kids class, social or otherwise, not by a long shot. My peer group hung on the fringes; we weren't great students, great athletes, or remotely popular. The only thing I was any good at was baseball, but like so many things in my life, I ended up quitting my senior year. Why? Because I was a quitter. I got benched for the first time in my life and couldn't take it. So I quit.

Looking back, I guess you could say my true claim to fame was disruption.

Maybe it was a way to attract attention. Maybe I was making up for what was missing at home. But my thing was turning a class upside down. All the teachers knew it, my classmates knew it, and so did I. It got to the point where people *awaited* my arrival the first day of every semester.

"All right!" cheered the boys.

"Ohhh, noooo," moaned the girls.

My finest hour had to be senior year when I rolled into the lot and parked my pride and joy, that bitchin' primer gray LTD, next to the Cadillac belonging to baseball buddy Leo James. I noticed smoke pouring out from under Leo's hood. So naturally I work my way over to Leo's class, about to make my grand entrance, when the teacher throws up a stop sign.

"Whoa, whoa," he says.

"But Leo . . . Leo," I say.

And the teacher goes, "Mr. Lopez, this is your problem. You just can't barge in here. You have no respect for my class. What you have to say to Mr. James you can say to the class."

So I say, "Class, Leo's car is on fire."

Now that's some funny shit. And it gets even funnier as Leo tears out of the room just as the fire trucks arrive. His Cadillac is like, totally, like oh, Hillary, totally engulfed in flames . . . along with the car next to it.

One whole side completely charred, one entire tire melted right to the ground.

Firemen scrambling around spraying foam and yelling, "Who owns this car? *Who OWNS this CAR?*"

Which is hysterical too, until I realize . . . *I own it.*

Had I not been brain dead I would have moved my pride and joy away from the towering inferno. Now my LTD was getting roasted right along with most of my stock: bottles of Seagram's 7 swiped from the Canyon Country liquor store where I worked on weekends and sold out of my trunk during Friday night football games. *Can you get TJ Swan? Absolutely, no problem, ese. What size?*

There remains one class door at SFHS that retains deep significance in my life. Port of entry into the class where one day—no joke—I walked in and told Mr. Shaffer, my twelfth-grade drama teacher, I wanted to be a comedian.

A stand-up artist in his own right, he'd proved good enough to work the Coconut Grove, but he wanted nothing to do with me or my dream. I can still see the dismissive smirk and hear the belittling tone after I told Mr. Shaffer.

"I don't have time to teach you," he scolded me in front of the entire class. "You know stand-up is an *art*."

So is sticking my foot up your ass.

Freddie had been dead for about two years, and some of the older brothers had turned to another cutting-edge comic. Which is how I discovered Richard Pryor, the next great influence in my life.

I remember the first time I saw him on ON-TV, a seventies Southern California cable service, doing his Long Beach concert *(Richard Pryor Live! in Concert)*. It was nothing less than a life-altering experience; a life preserver in a sea of personal emptiness and doubt, a big bright buoy from the opening scene: Pryor, stepping out of a limo, notebook in hand, striding up the stairs to the Terrace Theatre, then a quick cut onstage to this sharp-tongued genius dressed in red silk shirt, black pants and silver shoes. Like Freddie, it was like nothing I had ever seen. Pryor is black, but I didn't hear black. He was nothing less than a revelation—raw and real, so much stored-up pain yet so much damn humanity. And funnier than hell.

So when I found out Freddie loved Richard and Ron managed him too, I found a new hero.

I had Ernie run a copy of *Live! in Concert* on his VCR and I watched that sucker all day, every day. It literally became the background music of my life.

Eventually I would see *Car Wash, Silver Streak,* and *Which Way Is Up?* I purchased his books and albums. I even went so far as to drive by his house hoping to catch a glimpse of that canary Rolls-Royce of his pulling into the garage.

So it was, inspired by Pryor, that I wrote those words on that single slip of paper. About hitting the American people like a hammer. About being the best. Because, you see, just two months before I had attempted my most important first.

June 4, 1979. The Comedy Store Annex. Westwood, Calfornia.

Monday night, Open Mic night, in this little hole-in-the-wall

place Ernie and I had scouted for weeks. The kind of place where your name goes into a hat and the first ten names drawn get spots beginning at eight (Around ten, the regulars would come in and try out new material, guys like Howie Mandel, Bob Saget, and Gary Shandling.)

Ernie had been virtually living at the house, cowriting my material. When the big day finally arrives, we show up at five-thirty P.M., a full two and a half hours before the "draw," and I'm scared shitless, yet knowing full well, short of a stay by the governor, I was powerless to stop the fact that I was going onstage. To calm my nerves . . . Ernie and I do what any red-blooded, underage American male does when he's scared shitless: we rush over to the Westwood Ho and have a guy buy us a bottle of Boone's Farm, that all-purpose relaxer.

A couple of hours later, slightly buzzed and completely petrified, I go up in front of about forty-five people.

And I'm truly awful.

What comes out is nothing but degrading, horrible stuff, Mexicans and fake accents, 1970s shit, no sense of family or anything. I even stoop so low as to steal one of Freddie's jokes about running with a TV.

After three minutes of speaking—like an auctioneer on speed—I finally stopped to take a breath. That was the only laugh I got—at the end when I finally paused. People thought it was funny. Maybe it was.

Based on that "performance," Ernie and I decide to "retool" the act, which eventually leads to the One. Third time out, another Monday Night at the Annex, right after graduation. Only this time when I show up, the place is packed. We wait. And wait. And wait. Until ten-ten—the exact time—when Joey Gaynor comes up and says the two most frightening words I'd heard in my life: *"You're next."*

Next? I check my watch. *Next! Lo siento, señor, you must be mistaken, sir. Why would I be going on now?* But I do, after a guy named Billy Brown. He was a white guy whose big bit was about how Mexicans have small feet and that's why they walk funny. I turned to Ernie and

said, "I'm going to try something." I went onstage and opened with, "The guy before me did a bit on Mexicans having small feet. Now he knows different because I just shoved this one up his ass!" It got the biggest laugh of the night. It worked . . . everything worked.

The audience is laughing, actually *laughing,* sometimes so hard I have to *take time* between jokes to let them breathe. Afterward outside the club, everyone is on me—"Incredible!" "You have *got* to meet the lady from the Comedy Store!" "Where you playing next?"—and for the second time in my life I *feel alive.* The first jolt coming just fifteen minutes earlier up on that stage.

And you know the best part? Ernie taped the fucking show. Taped it, man, on a flip-top RadioShack Realistic recorder, me and Ernie running up and down Westwood Boulevard like a couple of dogs just released from the pound. I did it. And they laughed. *They laughed.*

Out of breath, we finally plopped down in the doorway of some medical building and listened to the tape.

That first time, it was like a blood transfusion. I don't think there'll ever be a high like that first comedic kiss—the injection of love, attention, acceptance, spirit flowing into my body, washing away my deadbeat dad, mom, life on Hager, along with Mr. Shaffer—you with the red hair and bangs wherever you are—and all those other doubters who told me that I can't do something.

That I am a Nobody.

Fuck 'em. Hit people with a hammer. Be the best.

Be Somebody.

FALSE STARTS

Why?

What could possibly drive a person to the Comedy Store on Monday nights or some dingy downtown bookstore for Open Mic Night? Why expose yourself to the agony of a failed punch line? Why try to learn a skill nobody can teach?

The answers come easier these days, especially when I'm standing in front of 7,500 adoring fans. But back in the day, the road to so-called stardom proved twisted and unwelcoming.

Far more often than not I'd sign up for an open mic night—and leave. My ten-minute spot due to start at, say, nine-twenty, and the closer it got to nine, the closer I got to ducking out the back door.

"I can't do it, man," I would tell Ernie, who was invariably at my side. "I just can't do it."

"Okay, then, let's go," he would say.

I guess I chickened out about half the time those first few months out of high school. One time at the Improv I even performed under the fake name E. A. Arlen. E. A. from Ernie Arellano and Arlen from the anglicized version of his last name.

"E. A. Arlen," said a guy named Howard, pulling my "name" out of a hat.

Well, if I fuck this up, at least I've got ol' E.A. to blame.

So I went up and did my thing—badly, I'm sure—although I do

remember one guy in the back yelling out, "All right, E.A.," as I left the stage. It was the only time I ever performed under an assumed name.

After humiliating myself on this and numerous other occasions, I quit comedy completely from March 9, 1980, to March 14, 1982. During this painful two-year period I watched Paul Rodriguez hammer *his* way into America's consciousness while I drifted, feeling sorry for myself, not terribly committed to anything or anybody—partying too much, playing a ton of local softball, hitting Ted Nugent concerts at the drop of a hat, unable to watch even local comics. It simply hurt too much.

Mostly me and Ernie just hung out. One day when we were nineteen we borrowed his brother's cherry '67 Chevy Impala to go to a record store. I thought Ernie was buying, and he thought I was, but neither of us had any money. So we came up with this plan where Ernie would grab some cassettes at a five-fingered discount, and I would be parked around the corner in his brother's car with the passenger door open for Ernie to jump in. So there I was sitting behind the wheel when here comes Ernie flying around the corner with his arms full of cassettes—only I couldn't get the car started. The clerk is hot on his trail, I am trying everything to fire up the getaway car, and Ernie runs right past me, looks back, lets the tapes fly, and just keeps running.

My first real run-in with a series of dead-end jobs began at the Wilshire Book Company, owned and operated by a guy named Melvin Powers. Some of you might recognize the name because one of the owners of the airplane parts factory on my show is named Mel Powers. I do that a lot: bring my personal past into my fictional present. It's my way of keeping it real. Reminding me of who I am and where I've been. (For those seeking further examples to impress friends and bartenders, my best friend on the show is named Ernie and the actual exterior of our TV house is actually just a few blocks away from my home on Hager. Actually.)

In real life, Mel Powers specialized in self-help books and tapes like *Think and Grow Rich* and *How to Win at Blackjack*. Not exactly

Nobel Prize–winning literature. My mistake was treating my job like a job: Every morning, I'd dutifully get dressed up, take in orders, fill boxes, and ship them to all corners of the globe with missionary zeal. Which was all fine and dandy until one day one of the guys in shipping said, in essence, "Hey, *ese,* what the fuck are you doing? You can come in at one and still get everything you need done."

Well, that's all I needed to hear, especially at $2.35 an hour.

So I started showing up late, which worked out great, until one day Mel came by with some Asian businessmen and played Big Shot, saying, "How's everything going, George," and me responding, equally Big, "Pretty good, Melvin." Well, the quizzical look on his face told me that perhaps the *Melvin* reference was a mistake. Sure enough, they let me go that afternoon.

So then I went off to a series of jobs arranged by Benny, who, as usual, was motivated purely by self-protection. She obviously wanted no part of me lying around the house all day watching *Live! in Concert* for the thousandth time and eating her out of house and home. But first she forced me to enroll in a course at L.A. Trade School in Woodland Hills. *"Mira, electronics is the future."* Maybe, but this class was set in the 1950s. Taught by this old guy, Mr. Holtz, who had a horrible temper, it was more like TV Repair 101 and filled with several *really* odd stoners. Picture the educational equivalent of the disability center my mom pulled her dates from, and you're batting a thousand. (I had hit the same percentage in computer class. Another bright idea from you know who. I went 1–1 in that game. One and done.)

So I'm doing my student thing at the trade school until one day my friend Kenny Ramirez got killed by a local police officer right in front of his house. He was unarmed. The LA *Daily News* ran a front-page story on the incident, and the next day Mr. Holtz held up a copy of the paper before making a remark that shot some fire up my ass.

"You know," he said, "these are the kind of kids who get what they deserve."

Get what they deserve? For those of you scoring at home I can actually count the number of times I've ever stood up and spoken up on one finger—that time the waiter hassled my grandfather in that restaurant. This was incident number two, and this time, I used the middle finger.

"Hey," I said. "That *kid* you're talking about was a friend of mine."

"Well, it says here," Holtz said, doing some pointing of his own, "that he had a kid out of wedlock and he was going to get married."

"What the fuck does that have to do with him getting shot?"

So I deleted Mr. Holtz, *pendejo,* and went to work nights at Tanden Magnetics making floppy discs for computers. Tanden was New Delhi West run by this Indian guy who was hiring anybody with a pulse. I quickly wore out my welcome there, moving on— once again, thanks to Benny—to Sperry Aviation. It was mindless fucking work, at night, all alone in a room. My job was putting one circuit board after another on a Fairchild 2000 tester, sucking it down, checking the connections, and printing a report. *Resistor C-4 needs to be replaced.* Then taking that little report and slapping it on the board before sending it on to the fine ladies in rework.

I turned twenty-one years old in that mind-numbing place, day in and day out testing those boards. Finally in March of 1982 it dawned on me: *I want to be a comedian and I work nights.*

So I went to my boss and told him the truth.

"I need your help," I said.

I guess at some point in his life George Martin wanted to be a musician and never followed his dream. So he understood mine. He immediately moved me to days working the back-room rewire area. The only downside was it contained a cast straight out of *Star Wars.*

There was a Russian dude who spent all his money at massage parlors and lived to tell us about it. One time he actually took a tape recorder in a paper bag and when he came back he played the tape for us—we could hear the paper bag rustling, the Asian masseuse, the negotiating, everything. The Russian was beside himself, so proud of his

little adventure. When he was ready to climax, all we heard was "Tiger! Tiger! Tiger!"

Tiger?

As the story goes, there was this picture of a tiger on the wall, and that's all the Russian could think of yelling. Guess what we called him from then on.

Then there was this guy, Chuck, who looked like George Gobel, and Ted, who did nothing but talk about his wife and ask about investments. And finally, there was Mary Graham.

I loved Mary. She could have been the first WNBA player, tall and pigeon-toed and talked real slooww, always starting with "I'm saying," especially when she ragged on Ted: "I'm saying, the only reason you talk about your wife so much is that's the only pussy you'll ever get." I used to sit and talk to Mary for hours, telling her what I wanted to do with my life.

I found the steno notebook I used to keep back then. The date—March 1, 1982—neatly noted in the upper-right corner of the cover with the desperate words nearby drenched in black ink: **THE COMEBACK!**

Inside the front cover, I wrote, *First time up since March 9, 1980,* and the sixteen pages that followed tell the story of a young man set on a mission to make it or break it. Sketches started and stopped; dates; times recorded right down to the second (5:40). Detailed reviews of major club appearances (*Improvisation, March 14, 9:55 P.M. Very good Audience*).

I'd left the land of Nobodies and for six straight months tried to break down that cultural barrier between Chicanos and those who see us as little more than dishwashers or hotel maids. To them I say, take a look around, mendijo, starting with the May 5, 2003, *Sports Illustrated* cover story naming the 101 Most Influential Minorities in Sports.

Take a gander at numero 5, Mr. Arturo Moreno. And I quote: "Out of nowhere, the Phoenix businessman jumped nearly to the top of our list last month by purchasing the world champion [Anaheim] Angels for $180 million, making him the first Latino majority owner in sports. Moreno, who made billions in the outdoor-advertising business, was partially attracted by Anaheim's potentially lucrative Latino fan base."

Just like I was in March of 1982, Latinos are *dale gas,* going for it, in every corner of this country—food, art, music, science, and everything in between. From Moreno to J.Lo to Eva Mendes to Jimmy Rodriguez to Angie Martinez to Cristina to Thalia, around the horn, baby, and back, we got it covered.

And that's just *ahora, puto* . . .

But I digress.

While the notebook routines centered on cultural targets within easy reach, like remembering the Alamo ("How could I forget? I couldn't sit down for a week"), the actual words meant little. Instead, it's all the dates that count: March 4, 12, 13, 19, 20, 21, and 27. For the first time in my life, after so many false starts, I was actually *working* at becoming a comedian. And little by little the words and images began to fall into place. Like the bit I called "Housewarming" that was written and buffed and polished from March until September 1982.

I'm really proud of the fact that we're the first
Mexican family to move into Mission Hills
    So as our neighbors found out—Hey, you're movin'
in . . . good, 'cause we're gonna throw you a
housewarming party
    So as the neighbors found out, hey, you don't mind if
we throw you a little housewarming party
    We were surprised
    We were *really* surprised because it took the fire
department more than five hours to put our *house* out

I stayed at Sperry for three years, until the company relocated to Arizona and I was laid off, which led to an interesting two-year stretch, in my mid-twenties, at a place called Teledyne in Northridge. By day I worked as assembler of computer equipment before a promotion to gopher, literally "going for" parts, "going for" signatures, all for the princely sum of eight bucks an hour, while writing and performing (and partying) at night. It was there, at Teledyne, I struck up this terrible relationship with a woman thirteen years my senior.

"Look, if you don't want me, just tell me right now," she said.

I didn't want her, but I couldn't do it. I couldn't tell her.

So instead I'm trying to leave her house and she's literally holding my ankle and I'm *dragging* her to the door.

But I can't say no. Because I couldn't say no to anything. Drank too much. Helped people I barely knew move from place to place. Why? Because—where is that Chicano choir again?—*I was afraid people were not going to like me.*

So guess what? I'm running completely on empty. And I start taking pills to stay awake. Nothing serious, just some whites to put a little more tiger in *my* tank. All fine and good until one day out of the blue this coworker comes up and asks me if I can get him some of the same shit I'm taking. "Sure," I say, "I can get you something." So I let him have a couple. A few days later he's back for more.

"Sure," I say. After all, I'm Mr. Big Shot, Mr. I Can't Say No. "How many more you want?"

"About a thousand."

"All right," I say. "Let me talk to my guy."

Like I've even got *a guy.*

From then on, every time I see *this guy* he's hounding me. "When am I going to get that jar, bro? *C'mon, bro. Where's the stuff?"*

"I'm talking to my guy, man, it's coming."

I never tell this guy there is *no guy.* That it's *never* coming.

Meanwhile, a coworker who happens to use my office and phone on the night shift is selling coke right under my nose. Now, I

think you know where this is headed: The phone is tapped. The guy hounding me for drugs is not a coworker. He's a cop working undercover. So when the shit comes down and they take me in, it's like junior high all over again, only the adult version.

"Did you know Steve was selling coke at night?" the coworker cop said.

Absolutely not.

"Are you sure?"

"Man, I work during the day. I don't know what the fuck happens at night."

So the cop grabs a folder and takes out a transcript about the size of the September *Vanity Fair* and says, "On November fourth, at three-thirty, did you discuss . . ."

"If it says so in the book, I guess I did."

So once again I get fired—the worst they can really do given the fact I didn't do shit—but not before people around the office start with *"So that's why he was so happy . . ."* and *"No wonder he was so funny."* I couldn't tell my grandmother. No way. So every day for weeks I get up, get dressed, and pretend to go to work. Until one day somebody calls to inquire what kind of stuff I was on.

"What do you mean?" my grandmother says. "He's not on any drugs. He's at work."

"No, actually, Mrs. Gutierrez, he doesn't work here anymore."

Uh-oh.

But I'll say this: For all the shit she did to me when I was a kid, she protected me when I needed her the most. She never told my grandfather about the drugs, but when he found out I had been fired, he threw me out of the house. Even asked for my key back.

"You don't live here anymore," he told me. "Now when you come over, you knock."

Holy shit. I don't know about you, but in a Mexican family that's like excommunication. You can't watch TV. You can't eat the food. You can't use the backyard weights. You can't bring home a woman.

So now that's me. No money. Sleeping on my friend Arnold's couch. Still trying to get away from that crazy older woman.

It was only after this, after everything was as shitty as it was going to get, that I finally began to commit to comedy.

And for the first time in my life I wasn't going to quit.

TEAM LEADER

When I was eighteen I went to work at a Fedco in Van Nuys. And they made me Team Leader. They gave a Chicano a vest that said "Team Leader" and I figured I was, like, Erik Estrada. I would just stand in my area, hands on hips, staring off into the distance, protector of all car-care products, until someone came up and asked how to get back to the front of the store, and then I would start all over, "Yeah, I can help you, I'm the Team Leader . . ."

Naturally, I was feeling pretty good about myself until I was sleeping one day and my grandma found my vest.

"Hey, sleeping beauty. What does this, what is this, this vest I found. Team Leader, what is that?"

"It means . . . I'm the leader of the team."

"What? I can't hear you, I can't hear you, what?"

"I'm THE TEAM LEADER!"

"Hey, lower your voice. Oh, you're the team leader. What about the underwear I found under your bed. Why you crying? You wanna see them? Follow me, vamos."

Every Mexican mother had a bucket with water and Clorox—for the shitty underwear. And a stick. So she started stirring: "Look at these, cabrón. Look at these. Mira, look at them! Two days, tiene caca. Look at that. It looks like you sat

on an Almond Joy, *cochino*. Look at that, Mr. Team Leader. Why you crying? Because I found the underwear! They found me! I should be the one who is crying! Look at that! I put Shout, and it shouted back! With a broom I had to sweep them outside."

No, but you're the team leader, *nombre*. Of what team? The Caca Team? Follow me with the brown dot! *Mira,* go, team!

COMMITMENT

OTHER VOICES—ERNIE ARELLANO

Those first five years, I went to practically every show. I helped craft the segues, noted the ad lib material that worked, and served as George's sounding board. George tape-recorded every show. One time I was in charge of the tape recorder, but when we went back to listen to it all you could hear was me rattling ice in my glass and chomping on ice through the entire set.

After a few more minor stops and starts, the last time I actually worked for a living was a three-year stint at the ITT plant in Van Nuys beginning in 1984. My boss was a sweet country guy with the sweet country name of Bob Bonner. It wasn't too long before ol' Bob realized that my mind was in a different place from aerospace.

"I can't let you get paid," he told me one day in his syrupy Southern drawl. "But if yawl want to, you can go out there on the road and come back and still have a job."

So that's exactly what I did. Hit the road for real in April 1986, quickly discovering how the road hits back. Early on, I was so jacked to tell jokes for a living—make that a *partial* living—I hardly noticed the beating. Sure, the telltale signs were there: the condos that looked

something out of MTV's *Spring Break,* and comedy club vans that smelled like piss. But back then the prospect of two weeks in Houston or Tempe seemed like paradise to me. I was barely making people laugh, but at least I was likable. People *wanted* to laugh; I just hadn't given them a real reason yet. I was more of a novelty—a Chicano doing stand-up, the minor league version of Paul Rodriguez, aka Pablo, who a couple of years earlier had made something of a name for himself on television. Now I'm like in his big brown shadow, which, for the moment, is not a bad thing to be.

I did exactly two weeks that first year, traveling to Houston twice, taping every single show. Writing every spare moment I could, working on my delivery. Working up to the day I could leave the aerospace "industry" for good. That day finally came on July 17, 1987, when, with $210 in my pocket and my *culo* slammed shut, I told sweet country Bob Bonner that I was done with ITT. I was ready to become a full-time comic.

It took another year of playing small clubs and dealing with small-minded club owners before I got signed by a couple of slick-dick agents that hung around the clubs, guys that I eventually left, and by February 1989 I had a fresh set of agents and the first real signs of hope. *The Arsenio Hall Show* had debuted the month before to immediate acclaim, and one night, while waiting to go on at the Improv on Melrose, Arsenio showed up to scout talent along with his producer and director. I was standing up against the wall when he walked in and walked right by without noticing, an attitude that changed once I went on stage and ripped into Linda Ronstadt and the emblem Sinéad O'Connor had carved into the side of her head. Arsenio came right up to me afterward and wagged a big finger in front of my face.

"I'm going to put you on my show," he said, and he did.

It was a couple of months later, May to be exact, that I met a rather interesting woman, Ann Serrano, at The Ice House. No major fireworks at first—just some interesting, humanitarian conversation

about the lack of Latinos on TV and the big screen—
a conversation we continued when she asked me to
close a comedy-night fundraiser she was doing for
the Latino Theatre Lab.

OTHER VOICES—ANN (SERRANO) LOPEZ

*Being a first generation Cuban-American has definitely shaped
my outlook on life. My mom, dad, sister, and grandmother had
come from Cuba with two bags and $800. They didn't even bring
clothes in their bags—they just brought pictures. They left their
country with their wedding rings; everything else, including all the
jewelry, stayed behind. Both my mother and father had medical degrees, so before they came to this country they wrote three hundred
letters to hospitals asking for employment. One hospital re-
sponded—Cook County Hospital in Hartford, Connecticut,
where I was born. Hard work is the Cuban mantra. I was brought
up on it.*

*I was a casting assistant to Dan Guerrero and we were hired
by Disney to do a national search for Latino comedians. All the
comedians were horrible, and then we got the tape of George.
Eventually I saw him onstage, and there was this purity about
him—an honesty. He was a middle act on his way to becoming a
headliner. He was still green but his comedy stood out because it
was insightful, not mean-spirited. It was racially relevant without
the chip on the shoulder. Or so I thought. I would discover he had
a huge chip.*

*It's interesting, because at this point he really glamorized his
childhood; he spoke about his grandmother as if she were the best
in the world. So when we started dating, I thought, having just lost
my grandmother, that God had sent me another grandmother. And
then I met her. I was, like, oh, my God, what is this? I didn't know
a Latino woman could be so negative.*

*I saw in George such a vulnerability, and no one
else saw it. There was something, I can't pinpoint it
exactly. There was a desire to do better. A drive. I was
brought up with the same thing. Striving to do better.*

I *was* doing better. By now I was making a couple of grand a week
and for the first time in my life got offered a part in a movie—the cult
fave *Ski Patrol*. But there would be no second act to my stand-up
start. No huge follow-up to *Ski Patrol*. Just a long, slow ten-year
descent to, if not the bottom of the barrel, at least the murky middle
between starving and stardom that sucked the life right out of me.

I was still getting good gigs—*Sunday Comics, Comic Strip Live,
Evening at the Improv* hosted by the somnolent Mr. T—but barely
making a name for myself outside Southern California. Not even fifteen shots on red-hot *Arsenio* got the phone ringing; I'd do a perfect
set and *nobody* would call, or least *nobody* who could lift me to the
level of my heroes, supply the sweet success of my dreams.

It was a complex and confusing time. By early 1990 and for the
next three years I rattled through an interesting series of personal
managers—Harvey "Broadway Danny Rose" Elkins, George Shapiro
and Howard West (Seinfeld's guys), Michael Green at Geffen—one
"name" bigger than the next, but nothing clicked. Much of my mis-
ery brought on by the fact . . . that I refused even to audition for the
stereotypical parts now coming my way: Chicano drug dealer, Chicano pimp, Chicano gang leader; you name it, I got offered to play it
Chicano-style. One time my agents brought me a script of this gang
leader with "a heart of gold," and I'm like, he's still a gangbanger, I'm
not doing it. Foolish me, I wanted to make it without the Latino
crutch. I wanted to be somebody special. The only part I got was as a
detective in the movie *Fatal Instinct* in 1993, a title that should go on
my tombstone because my refusal to play type cost me my agents,

who, after one turndown after another, said sorry, we're letting you go. Which would have been fine had I not just returned from putting one hundred head shots listing them as my reps in the slot at the post office. I should have shot myself.

Why not? By the early nineties I was essentially a dead man anyway. No agent, no manager. I took to watching *Rocky*. Hell, I *was* Rocky. Nobody wanted me. Unless, of course, you count Ann.

OTHER VOICES—ANN LOPEZ

The early nineties were the Arsenio Years. His show was the "it" place to be in Hollywood. Madonna, Tom Cruise, Bill Clinton, every rapper known to man, Mike Tyson, Prince . . . they all graced his stage. It was the show to do.

You could feel the electricity in the air the moment you walked onto Stage 29 at Paramount. The green room was the place to see and be seen. George went on to do the show more than any other comedian. Arsenio and Joy Dulce, the senior talent coordinator, came to rely on George as the guy they could always count on to be funny. If they had a controversial show—like the time they had Ice T explaining the lyrics of his song "Cop Killer"—they called George. If a guest canceled at the last minute, they called to see if George was in town. If they needed a funny behind-the-scenes taped piece—they called George.

Comedy was king and there were a myriad stand-up comedy shows on the air. George did them all and did them often: Comic Strip Live, Sunday Comics, VH1 Comedy Hour, *MTV's* Half Hour Comedy Hour, Evening at the Improv, *just to name a few. It was also the time of the "revolving door" of talk shows—Suzanne Somers, Rolanda, Tempestt Bledsoe, etc. All*

the talent coordinators knew George and booked him on their shows. If they moved to a new show, George was one of the first guests they booked.

George and I were now a business team as well as a couple. It had become painfully obvious that George's vaudevillian management had become ineffective and embarrassing. After a bitter and sad parting with his manager Harvey Elkin, I worked as George's manager/publicist. I was sending out letters and tapes to the top managers, doing his publicity, and calling all my casting director friends and contacts. I booked George on shows that my partner and I were producing. He opened for Bob Hope and Joel Grey and warmed up the audience for our Fox television special Ray Charles: 50 Years in Music. I was relentless. I was in the George Lopez business. I loved him, I respected him, and I wanted him to succeed.

But this was also a frustrating time. George would kill on these shows and the phone would not ring. He was everywhere on TV and gaining recognition, but that didn't translate into money in the bank. These shows pay a SAG or AFTRA designated rate that at the time was about $600 or $700, with residuals being considerably less.

I think George had a lot of anger over the fact that people were labeling him a Latino comedian, and he was just trying to be a comedian. People don't label Jerry Seinfeld a Jewish comedian. Minorities are the only ones they label.

I used to tell George, "If you were white or black, you'd have a show. They don't know what to do with you. Look what happened to Margaret Cho—they tried to make her something she wasn't." I think George had a chip on his shoulder being compared to Paul Rodriguez, who was not the kind of comedian George was or is. George is more in the vein of Dick Gregory or Bill Cosby, but because both he and Paul are Latino, George became the other Latino comic. A lot of people were loyal to Paul. And now there were George and Paul. To some that meant there was room for only one. Although there's room for twenty black comedians.

My immigrant Cuban background kept me positive. I was used to being the underdog. I pushed George and I cheered him on. But I had no idea of the depth of George's depression and self-destructive behavior. He was falling deeper and deeper into a dark hole and the love of a Type A Cuban cheerleader wasn't what was going to get him out.

To this day I'm not entirely sure why Ann stuck around, given that I'd had no interest in a "relationship" beyond man's most basic needs. Love and intimacy were foreign words to me. Thanks to my mother and grandmother, I had no interest in being loved or giving love; had no idea what it meant to be close with a woman, to share. No idea how to take even the first step in that direction.

Which is why, in December 1992, after about two years of dating, and living together for a year Ann was forced to speak up.

"Guess who's getting married?"

"Who?"

"Us."

"Really? When?"

"Next September."

"All right, let me know. I'll be there."

And that's all I basically said. Okay. Have at it, girl. And while you're at it, don't forget to buy your own ring.

That's the kind of man I was, the kind of hole I was in.

The Angriest Most Depressed Man Alive. That's what I called myself.

By 1995, that little boy who grew up dreaming about becoming Somebody was long gone, replaced by a man who told jokes to half-

empty rooms. I was back to being a nobody, believing once more that nothing special was ever going to happen to me.

Despite making a six-figure salary, I was struggling to pay the bills, struggling to keep the road from chewing me up. It just gets *old*. In and out of your wife's life every three or four days. Gone every weekend. Constantly being second-guessed by club owners while trying to hold the attention of people out to drink and party and forget. If you're a musical act you don't have to worry about holding anybody's attention—you just play over it. But in comedy, noise is a distraction; it weighs on your brain. And in most cases the weight of your self-worth is so low to begin with that any criticism or inability to entertain just buries you. And angry and buried I was.

Maybe I looked sharp in jeans and jacket in one set, black suit and T-shirt in the other, maybe my voice was deeper and cockier, but in the end what I was doing in 1995 was the same old shit from three years before. The same tired old El Torrito fast-food "Run-for-the-Border" Taco Bell "Menu Mentality" bullshit. Sure, there are some strong moments—my body language and facial expressions were better, and there's a glancing reference to Biff and Muffy—but my set essentially offered no originality whatsoever, no attempt to drill down or open up. All in all, about as impersonal an act as an act could be.

I was going into cities like Austin and San Antonio and hearing how great all the *other* comedians were when they came to town. Meanwhile, I'm staying at the Residence Inn being shuttled around to these tiny little Mexican radio stations the day of the show, desperately attempting to drum up business. And knowing full well that when I walked on stage more than three-quarters of an 1,100-seat theater would be empty.

I remember going to Kansas City and telling the guy who was

opening for me, "God, if I could just do my fucking act." But I couldn't. Because I didn't have an *act*. In the back of my mind I had an idea, but I just didn't trust it enough to let people, these strangers, in. I couldn't make myself vulnerable in places like K.C. or Indianapolis. I thought people would find it painful or boring—or, God forbid, both.

Actually, my worst experience came in downtown Indy after the first of three Saturday shows where I bit it so bad that afterward I just walked outside and thought about walking home. From the get-go the seven o'clock audience was half dead, the place so quiet I could hear the words ringing inside each and every head: *This guy is not funny. This guy is not . . .*

I swear it got so bad that for the first time in my life I taped notes on the top of a stool. And even *that* didn't help; my nerves were so shot I couldn't pick out a single word. The only thing I could see was this big-ass clock counting down every last second of my so-called act. Twenty-five lousy minutes, me waiting for the big hand to hit the seven, and every damn time I looked up it'd be at the two with me thinking, *Shit, what am I going to do?*

Leave town, that's what. Take my sorry ass back to California and get a real job. But I couldn't, I just couldn't, so I stuck it out, bombing in all three shows, forced to suffer two more days before facing the firing squad again on Tuesday night. All I did on that Sunday and Monday was sit in this dark, dinky, stinky-ass hotel room and watch TV and think: I died last week and I'm gonna die this week. The only time I left was to eat at McDonald's. I never felt so alone and lonely in my life. So damn sad I went to the pay phone in the lobby and called my *grandmother*.

It wasn't long after the Indianapolis experience that a critic in Orange County felt compelled to call my show "mundane." "Mundane" is

not a good word for comedians. I remember reading the review and asking myself, "Is it mundane?" and the answer was yes. But by 1997 that's exactly what I had become—completely ordinary. Making good coin, about $13,000 for eight or nine shows, but living a life I had come to hate: Partying and drinking in the club afterward, away from home for ten days at a time. It was brutal, man, the alarm going off at five-thirty in the morning, signaling another week in Chicago or up in San Francisco or Sacramento.

"You know what, Ann?" I said one day. "I'm exactly what I never wanted to be. A road comedian. Making my living by being away."

"But we're not struggling," she said.

"Ann, I've got to send my fucking check home on Monday after the Sunday show FedEx so you can put it in the bank on Tuesday. That's *not struggling?* I've got to call you and tell you I just put the check in the mail. *That's not struggling?*"

I was destroying myself. Ann doesn't even know the degree to which I was destroying myself. I don't quite know what all the alcohol and dark nights were masking; I guess I simply didn't like myself. Or my selves, because there really were two Georges: the one on stage whom everybody saw, and the one hidden backstage who wanted to be recognized but wasn't.

Today, Ann is so important to me. She is the person who through it all stayed true. Even in the darkest times she never broke. I know some things still bother her, but I have done all the apologizing I can do. That's the thing about Ann: She strengthens my weakness with unconditional love and commitment.

OTHER VOICES—ANN LOPEZ

I kicked him out of the house. I jam-packed his Volvo with everything he owned and sent him to our condo. I found out he was

George and grandfather
Refugio Gutierrez (1971).

George, Grandma Benny,
grandfather Refugio Gutierrez, and
his grandfather's father (1971).

Grandfather Refugio Gutierrez and George (1971).

George in Mexico (1971). Feeding a lamb with grandfather.

George *(back row, third from left)* and Little League baseball team (1973).

Learning to play bass in my bedroom (1978). I'm really a rocker at heart!

The one week I was *THIN*. Pismo Beach, 1983. Maybe the only picture of me without a shirt!

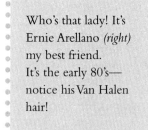

Who's that lady! It's Ernie Arellano *(right)* my best friend. It's the early 80's— notice his Van Halen hair!

First head shot (1985).

Wedding day: September 18, 1993.

Bread & Roses premiere, Cannes, France (2002). *(Left to right)* Ann Lopez, Elpidia Carrillo, director Ken Loach, Pilar Padilla, George, Adrien Brody.

Skiing in Aspen with Ann (1992). *El más chingón.*

Dancing on the fairway! I have arrived! My adopted hometown Pebble Beach . . . there goes the neighborhood!

The passion I have for golf is frightening. "It's in the eyes Chico."

The cast of the *George Lopez* show (2004). *(Left to right):* guest star J. B. Gaynor, Luis Armand Garcia, Valente Rodriguez, George Lopez, Constance Marie, Belita Moreno, and Masiela Lusha.

George and daughter, Mayan Lopez (2003).

pretty much leading a double life the first six years of our marriage. I was devastated. But as I looked at our marriage more closely, I realized my mistake was in not making him accountable for a lot of things, not making him take responsibility. Because of his childhood, I made excuses for him.

When I found out he was lying to me for so many years I seriously considered divorce. But for our daughter, I decided to try therapy. Our therapist made me realize the behavior wasn't toward me. It was toward himself. George was truly trying to destroy himself. He didn't believe he could have the life I offered him. He didn't believe someone could love him. He didn't believe he could have that intimate a relationship with another human being.

I had to take myself out of the equation. Ultimately I had to allow him to try and redeem himself and make himself whole.

I didn't understand in the beginning why it wasn't working. Why he wasn't further along. It was because of the demons of his childhood. But when he finally dealt with those demons through therapy that is when all his success happened. When he finally cleaned up his act, when he finally committed to family and being a better person, all of a sudden doors began to open.

I am so proud of George. I am in awe of all that he has accomplished as a man, as a husband, as a father, and as a performer. He has my heart para siempre.

I came home from the road to find my Volvo loaded with my clothes. She'd packed my car and left. So I drove to the condo near Universal Studios that we were trying to sell, unloaded my stuff, then went to Long's Drugs and bought a can opener, a pot, some soup, and diet soda. The place had no furniture or cable TV, so I bought a TV-VCR combo and watched movies on the floor. I slept on a rollaway bed.

It had always been about me in our relationship, then we had Mayan and it was still about me. But when I was living in that condo and everything was gone except her crib, disassembled in her room, I started to think: This is where we met. This is where our baby was born. It was so quiet in there, so empty, that I had a chance to think about what was really important, what I'd been missing, what the word "family" might actually mean. I stayed in that condo for about a month, and then I went home—a different man.

Not long after that, the turning point of my career came, not surprisingly, in New York City. I'd done five minutes down by the Seaport a few years before that had gone over like an oil tanker; I'd been intimidated by the scene, the city, Manhattan's prove-it-to-me mentality. This time the venue was big time—Caroline's—and afterward a friend from *Saturday Night Live,* Chris Rock's manager, Dave Becky, stopped into my dressing room.

"Do you mind if I give you some criticism?" he said.

"Fire away," I said.

"Well, I thought you were funny, but there's nothing in your act that tells me anything about you. What you like, dislike. You need to do what guys like Chris do. You know what he likes, what he doesn't like, how he *feels* about things."

He was right.

That's when I started to change. Started looking more and more at my life, my grandmother and family. The little boy in me. How mean my grandmother was. How everybody's always late. The lamp with the bad cord. I committed. And it started to hit.

By now my biggest problem was I had laid down a foundation of people who couldn't help me. People who could do me no good except take money for my dates. They were happy with me flailing around as a road comic. And I was so caught in the wash I wasn't aggressively pursuing representation. I didn't have an in. It's hard to get a manager off a straight "hello?"

I knew that Ron had managed Freddie. I'd seen his name on the back of Freddie's *Looking Good* album, the one he'd recorded live at Mr. Kelly's in Chicago. When I finally met Ron, I said, "Was Hunga Rican Productions out of your office?" And he said yes. I used to say to myself, *I wonder where Ron De Blasio is, and I wonder if he would think I'm funny.*

OTHER VOICES—RON DE BLASIO

It was March of 1998. We needed a comic to open for Vikki Carr in Cerritos. I tried to make a deal with George. He wanted a helluva lot of money. I thought he had a lot of balls. He didn't have to draw anybody; it was a sold-out gig. I called him. He wasn't returning calls. I persevered and continued to call him. Finally, he returned my call. I told him what we needed: thirty-five minutes, it had to be clean, had to be for white people, appeal to some Latinos but not a lot, had to be for both young and old.

He did it, and I went in and clocked it. Thirty-five minutes and he never even sneaked a look at his watch. Everybody liked him—and with that audience, some are well beyond retirement age, between seventy-five years old and death, and they were laughing. The Latino people got it. The kids who were there got it.

The interesting thing was I couldn't figure out how somebody, quite honestly, that talented, that good, I hadn't heard of. A guy this funny, quick, and clean and charming—where's he been?

So after the show I went backstage. You know, "Jeez, you looked pretty good."

So George said, "Are you working with comics?"

I said, "No, I'm working with music."

He said, "Oh."

I thought about it. This is interesting, but can he measure up with what I left, with all the great comics I had worked with before?

My instincts were right. But what puzzled me—I couldn't get over the fact—wait a minute, a guy that funny, that good, there must be a chink in the armor someplace. Why is he doing this?

MEDICINE . . . MEXICAN STYLE

*L*atino people, we never go to the doctor. We could be coughing blood, and still we won't go.

Other folk . . .

"Oh, God."

"What's the matter, Chance?"

"I don't know, Brogan. I have a scratchy sensation I'm not familiar with. Oh, my God, I better go schedule an MRI . . ."

My uncle had a head comin' right out the side of his neck. And he wouldn't go. The thing had its own pulse and hair and everything, and he still wouldn't go. You would tell him, "Hey, why don't you go get that checked?" and he'd get all mad.

"Get what checked?"

"Get what?"

"I didn't hear you, eh. Get what checked? I'm right here, *puto*. Get what?"

So you point at his neck.

"What, my—what, this? What—what is? What, *ese*? Who told you?"

Who told me? The HEAD told me.

"Hey, if you don't like it, don't look at it."

And your family encourages you not to go: "Mira, don't go, mira. If I were you, I wouldn't go. Because sabes que they're gonna find something wrong with you. Have you drank the 7UP? Drink it, all of it. The 7UP. *Mira*, it's gonna burn, *porque como tienes* carbohydrates, *pero*, drink it. And burp it up, *mira*. Because two years ago I had leukemia, *munchingo un Esprite*. With a lemon. And *sí*, look at me now, *mira*."

We may not go to the doctor, but we will go to the emergency room. And when we do, the entire family goes too. They won't go to a baptism or a wedding. But get into a car accident, and they're all there—drinking beer in the parking lot, yelling up at the windows.

"Ruben!"

"He probably can't hear."

"RUBEN!"

"He's in a coma."

"Is he dead?"

"No, he's not dead."

"Shit, you told me he was dead. We'd better return his TV."

The whole family will parade inside the hospital, and that's usually when the doctor comes out: "Oh, goodness. Are you all immediate family? This is quite a turnout. I've never seen a barbecue grill in the ER before. But the *carne asada* does smell fantastic . . ."

Your grandmother is over in the corner already lighting candles and praying with all her little friends when the doctor approaches.

"*Señora?*"

"*No hablo inglés. No hablo Englesh.* Doctor, *excusa* me, Doctor. I no talke too mush. I only been in United States fifty-nine years. I no talke too mush."

That's why we all have a spokesman for the family, the one who's the most educated. That's the one they call.

"Oscar!"

"*Cabrón*, talk to the doctor, *porque* you work at Target. Put your vest on. Why you crying? Put your vest on."

And there's Oscar with his red vest with the target on the back, using the big word that all Mexicans overuse: "Basically, we came to find out the basics, *ese*. From the basic standpoint."

Doctor: "Well, the situation is very grim."

"Hey, hey, slow down. I work nights, *ese*. I'm still in orientation . . ."

"*Well, the situation is grim. We've done some diagnostic work and his blood pressure is high and his hemoglobin level is incredibly low.*"

Now your grandmother decides to quiz Oscar: "*Qué, qué, mijo* something about he's feeling a lot of pressure *porque sabes que* the—the—the—homogoblins. *Joto,* homo goblins? They're gay goblins? That he's feeling pressure *porque* gay goblins?"

"*We've tried everything,*" *says the doctor.*

"Have you tried Vicks?"

"What?"

"My grandmother wants to know if you've tried Vicks. On the chess . . ."

One time my uncle had a heart attack, and the only people around were two- or three-year-old kids. And that's why you gotta teach your kids how to answer the phone. Sometimes, we encourage them not to— "Hey, let it ring. *Mira,* let it ring."

You ever watch Inside Edition *and in Kentucky, man, there's this little four-year-old kid who helps deliver a baby?*

"9-1-1 Emergency."

"Oh, hi. My mother's having a baby, I'm four. She's eight centimeters dilated. She's crowning."

But the kids who lived in my neighborhood, they don't know shit. So my uncle was lying on the couch, panting—"Ay, ay, ay"—and the kids are teasing him. "Ay, ay, ay, ay."

"I got a pain in my chess. I can't breathe. Tell your *tía, cabrón,* tell her I got a pain in my chess and I can't breathe!"

So you rush out in the backyard and there's your aunt talking to the lady next door with the fence in between them. And you're just standing there because they tell you not to interrupt. So you're just there—

"What do you WANT?"

"Tata says he has an ice chest and beef."

"'*Tás loco.* Lemme see."

So she huffs her way inside. And let me tell you, my uncle treated his wife horribly, all the time telling her she was lazy, while he was working all day. But when he had the heart attack, he was at her mercy.

"What's the matter?"

"I got a pain in my chess and I can't breathe."

"Oh, NOW you need me. Because you got a pain in your chess and you can't breathe. What's the matter? I can't hear you."

"*I got a pain in my chess . . . and I CAN'T BREATHE!*"

"Lower your voice, *cabrón!* I'm right here. Don't be yelling at me, 'cause I'm in control here, *cabrón,* Mr. I-Got-A-Pain-In-My-Chess-And-I-Can't-Breathe.

"Huh? Is that what's wrong? Because it didn't hurt you last night when you were dancing with that bitch in the backyard. Get that bitch to help you. Maria. *Cómo se llama la cabrona?* Stay like that! Stay like that! Don't call nine-one-one. Put the phone down, Raymond! Leave him like that! Leave him like that until he learns! I don't want the fire department knowing my life. Put the phone down . . ."

BIG BREAKS

I first met Cheech Marin in 1981 at a celebrity basketball game. Today he's one of the strongest influences in my life and one of my very best friends.

As any even semiserious stoner can tell you, back in the seventies Cheech and partner Tommy Chong were both *mas chingón* and together turned comedy into high art. Their classic *Up in Smoke* album and brilliant "Where's Dave? Dave's not here, man" routine alone are worth trips to the Hall of Fame. The biggest score for Cheech these days, however, is the one attached to a little white ball; he and I both love the game of golf and often play together on Sundays at a club called Saticoy near Somis. As I've said, anytime you get to hit something white with a club, how bad can it be?

As we tee it up and smoke a few cigars and walk the once-fertile farmland, the irony of a different kind of drive is not lost on either one of us. All along the Ventura Freeway, row after row of migrant workers are stooped at the waist, picking strawberries in the early-morning sun. Between botched shots and "breakfast mulligans," Cheech and I often find ourselves pondering with heartfelt pride the dizzy heights to which two *vatos* have climbed in show business—a place where Cheech often says "the tide" has rolled in and out on so many Latinos over the years. Cheech often recounts going to award shows and seeing people like Jimmy Smits, Hector Elizondo, and

Benjamin Bratt, strong, big-time actors, but the next year, everybody is gone. The tide rolling away.

Today Cheech lives at the beach in Malibu and I just bought a home along the magnificent 17 Mile Drive up near Pebble Beach. So we *know, ese.* We know what's passed before: We know, in many ways, this is our time; our tide is in and we are symbols of success and, in many minds, carrying a culture in Hollywood. We know that acting with pride and honoring our heritage are the best ways to pay tribute to those whose work, although seen by less, means as much or more.

So, you see, it's not surprising that it was Cheech who gave me the best advice when I was struggling against the tide. Get That One Thing, he told me, and turn That One Thing into Another Thing. He'd moved from hit albums to hit movies to a hit series. If I wanted to be part of a next wave of Latino stars, I needed That One Thing.

I found it in the garbage. Or, rather, it found me.

It was a movie directed by a Brit named Ken Loach. It centered around a janitors' strike—thus, the garbage—in Los Angeles. Without Ann, I would have turned down the audition for a union-busting manager at a downtown office building, just like I'd turned down countless others, figuring, what the fuck, what chance have I got? In this case I cared even less, having just returned from one more grueling weekend on the road.

It was late Sunday night when I walked in the house and she told me about the movie and the audition the next day.

"I ain't going," I said.

"Yes, you are," she said.

"I'm fucking tired, Ann," I said. "I just got home from San Francisco. Forget it."

But I'm up against the persuasive powers of Mrs. Lopez, so I end up going. Naturally there's no script, and Mr. Loach, when I finally get to meet him, makes Clint Eastwood look positively chatty.

"Where you from?" he finally says.

"From the Valley," I say. "And I know unions because I've worked in a factory or two (or three), and my grandfather worked hard, busted his ass for thirty years."

"Splendid," says Mr. Loach.

In due time another actor arrives, a talented guy named Greg Montgomery, and we proceed to run this scene: I'm the boss and he's the driver and he's given me some bad information. When we finished I thought Greg had nailed it, but Loach must have seen a moment or two from me he liked. So I got the nod. Greg got a "thank you."

"Now, whatever they tell you, you don't believe it," says Loach. I head into round two, a scene I'm supposed to improvise with two actresses. Loach tells me, "She's been late a number of times and you're tired of it."

So the woman walks in and I start right in.

"Where the fuck have you been?"

"I'm sorry," she says.

"We're running a fuckin' business here—where the fuck have you been?"

"My kid is sick."

"Your kid is sick. Listen, I got a lot of fuckin' sick kids myself, and I'm here. Your job is to work, not to fuck around."

So she starts crying, I've really hurt her, but I don't care. Something quite personal is at work here.

"Okay, okay, okay," says Loach.

Now the other actress walks in. I've turned my back to her.

"Sit down," I snarl.

When I finally spin around, she's down, and I tear into her like more than a few of my bosses have torn into me. Next thing I know, *she's* in tears.

"Okay, okay, okay," Loach says.

"Want me to do it again?" I offer.

"No, no, that's plenty," Loach says before uttering four more words, absolute lifelines to a dying man.

"We'll be seeing you."

I couldn't get to the car and phone home fast enough. "I think I've got this part," I told Ann. And sure enough, by the time I got home, I had it.

That movie, *Bread & Roses,* would open to critical acclaim at the Cannes Film Festival. Imagine that: This abused, neglected kid, who hated the color of his skin, who found quiet comfort in television, was headed to Cannes. Only I no longer had to imagine. Because suddenly, for this Chicano, it was true.

My next big break came courtesy of Rick Dees, whose morning show on KISS-FM in LA is the radio equivalent of a guest shot on Leno or Letterman. I did the show, and for some reason Rick and I got to ragging on Roy, his general manager, and out popped, "I didn't know the devil had a mullet head and chest hair that comes out of the top of his shirt." That pretty much put Rick on the floor.

It also put Roy on the phone to my publicist, asking if I would consider a job in radio.

Hell, yeah, Roy, I'd consider it. Considering I was sick and tired of dragging my ass out on the road. *Considering* I had nobody else knocking on my door.

In January 2000 I hit the airwaves for Clear Channel Communications at KCMG (MEGA 92.3) in Los Angeles, becoming the first Latino morning DJ to headline an English-language station in a market dominated by Spanish-language radio. As the new "team leader" of the morning lineup, you'd have thought I would have received a hug, a hello, a coffee mug, something. Instead all I got was frozen out . . . made to feel like Michael Jordan at his first NBA All-Star game.

I took shit for three days before bracing Roy. "Hey," I said. "Fuck this. I can't work with these dudes—they won't even let me talk, and everytime I do they roll their eyes. Is that why you got me in here?"

Not really, so eventually it's left for me to confront the Morning Guy, who's been there for thirty years, and his sidekick, Morning Girl. Faced with a rather *loco* Lopez, they both bail, leaving the door wide open. I charge right in and turn morning drive, from five to nine A.M., into a loopy free-for-all. My favorite time of the show was always the first hour when it was just me, the bus drivers, and the delivery guys—the real people—shooting the breeze over the air. In eight months, in the most competitive radio market on earth, I took the station from number twenty-two in the market to nine. I gave the station an identity and a presence. What I got in return was . . .

Fired.

That's what.

Because the climb wasn't fast enough, my appeal not broad enough for a new *pendejo* program director, truly the wet blanket of comedy, the human water bucket you keep by the campfire.

But I got over it. Because the one radio thing had already given way to Another Thing. A week after being fired I was on the cover of *Variety,* having signed a big development deal.

For a show that simply changed my life.

OTHER VOICES—RON DE BLASIO

The more people I asked about George, the more incomplete their answers were. So I told him, "I want you to tell me the name of every person you've ever spoken to who said he likes you and is in some position of power or had some position of power at that time."

I went waaay down the list of everybody and called every single one. Nothing. "Oh, yeah, he's a smart guy. He's a good guy. But if he was really good somebody would have picked him up by now. He's not a kid anymore."

I didn't like the word I kept hearing: Latino
comic. *Yes, he had a lot of Latinos in his audience, but
I also found out that he was considered among comics
to be the most versatile, the most eloquent. I went to
work.*

Thanks to Ron's hard work, by the summer of 2000 my stand-up
career had hit another gear—I was headlining bigger and better clubs,
filling small arenas, and making a name for myself with a powerful
group of promoters. Yet, as often happens, less meant more. For me, it
was a performance in August, in one of the classic Southern California haunts, the Improv in Brea.

By this time I'd been on the circuit full-time for more than fifteen years. No longer was I mundane. There was a swagger now, a
rhythm and a power to my one-hour-and-ten-minute show. The audience saw a man in a suit who entered the stage not with loud intro-
ductions anymore but to "Low Rider" by WAR, the group that was
with me in my car when I was alone and had nothing. But now
thanks to Dave Becky, Chris Rock's manager, and Ann, and some
soul-searching, finally, right from the start, I had something to say.

*"Now I'm going to warn you guys, I'm going to be speaking Spanish. So a lot
of you who don't understand, lo siento, I'm sorry, but what the fuck you
waitin' for? You think we're going BACK to Mexico? We're bringin' Mexico
here!*

*"It ain't like in Irvine where it's a forty-dollar fine if you speak Span-
ish. In Irvine, 'Mira, 'tá caliente.' 'Oh, my God. Nine-one-one? Hi. Hurry.
Oh, yeah, hurry, they just habla habla. Hurry! I don't know his name, I can't
read his neck.'*

"Look at the cholos not laughing. 'Eh, that shit ain't funny, vato. That's fucked up. That's a birf mark, ese. B-I-R-F.'

" '. . . Oh, my God . . . Oh, my God . . . And it looks like he's been crying. He has a teardrop under his eye . . .' "

It was Chris Rock who said that a comedian is someone who says, "Did you see that? That *ghost*." A comedian is the guy who sees things in ways nobody else does. Good things about people, bad things about people. And that's what I was *seeing* now, those ghosts of my mixed-up past and all the crazy characters who make up *mi familia*, who are out in society, and fusing them all together in a way that would make Prinze and Pryor proud.

I had a word for what was happening now. I called it Jazz comedy. Like Miles or the Duke, the notes are never the same. I was playing by feel, always in control, holding the crowd on a string. The radio gig, the movie, and the clubs were feeding off each other now, one espresso shot of confidence after another. I'd found a voice and a home for *"Oh, my God, Hillary,"* for *"Memmer? . . . U Memmer!"* for "Different Peoples" and "Backyard Weddings." I'd tapped deep into the grandmother lode, and on that night at the Improv, unbeknownst to me, Sandra Bullock was there to see it.

OTHER VOICES—SANDRA BULLOCK, ACTOR, EXECUTIVE PRODUCER, GEORGE LOPEZ

My partner, Jonathon Komack Martin, and I were in the process of getting some TV projects together, and we started talking about the lack of Latino and Asian presence on television, not a single show you can point to. I didn't really know why that was; some people talked about a lack of talent. I was tired of everything being white-washed on TV, so my partners and I spread out and attempted to hunt down every actor, Latino or Asian, and what we found was

there were problems finding great comedic talent, until we came across George.

His life, his stand-up—I just thought, This guy is unbelievable. Bittersweet, pushes the envelope, not always pleasant to hear, but with so much honesty, so effortless, people don't realize how easy he made it look.

Once I saw his act, I thought, Oh, my God, his situation, his life, is better than any idea we had!—an actual history like a train wreck and brave enough to share it.

I went to see George, and I met with him and Ann afterward. I was so excited—my problem is I don't think, I just talk sometimes, and I kept saying, "We have to do it! We have to do it now! I'd love to work with you."

I would bring in all my friends to see him—gay, straight, black, yellow, white—and see if they would react like I did, always assuming that I'm insane. And they would say, "This is the most amazing person. Why hasn't he been found earlier?"

So I have this lawyer, he's a little crazy, and he said, "Let me think of who I know," and Bruce Helford's name came up, and we thought, "Well, that man's insane; he'd be good to talk to." So I called him up and said he had to go see George and made him drive out to The Ice House.

Well, he saw George, and I went into Bruce's office and convinced him to shepherd the show. He had a lot of shows to handle, but he ended up saying he would see what he could do. In the end, Bruce's relationship with Warner Bros. and my deal with Warner helped. We discussed and begged a little and they got involved.

Outside of Ann, I owe everything to Sandy because she didn't have to do this. She's a major movie star, and even after her agents told her, "We really don't see a show here," she never gave up. She championed the idea of a network show and recruited the likes of Bruce Helford, who created *The Drew Carey Show* and had been a head writer for *Roseanne,* as my cocreator and executive producer. She understood that I was the kind of "package" that scared network execs—blessed with what someone once called "the face of a pit boss at an Indian casino." But Sandy had other ideas.

"Let me worry about the network," she told me. "You just worry about being funny."

What always impressed me the most about Tim Allen, Drew Carey, Paul Reiser, Ray Romano, and Jerry Seinfeld is that their sitcom success came from hammering away in the clubs for years. These guys were emotionally invested in their shows, which, in essence, were televised versions of their lives. You can't fake it much in television anymore, at least not in good television. People want to invest emotionally in stories and characters, and it doesn't matter if you're speaking English or Spanish or Spanglish, as long as you connect with your audience.

But did I have what it takes to make that connection? Could I cross over?

Sandy believed I could. So did her partners: Helford and—this gets a bit freaky—Jonathon Komack Martin, the son of *Chico* creator James Komack.

Now all we needed was a script.

To that end I spent much of the late summer of 2000 in my office at home watching—courtesy of the Time-Life collection—every single episode of *Sanford and Son,* six in a row, then another tape, and another. Not because I needed to laugh; no, what I needed to do was learn. About characters and how to play the physical side of comedy on a small screen, how you fire an insult and how to respond to that insult, how to introduce a neighbor—all the little nuances of

television that make the difference between personal and processed.

I didn't want my show to feel *manufactured*. I think people respond to the show because I'm a real person, a regular guy with all the nicks and cuts of anyone who has struggled to get by. I think people relate to that realness. Originally, Bruce wanted to write the pilot but once I started to talk, he said, forget it, you talk, we'll listen. And that's what I did for days on end, opening up in a room with Bruce and producer Robert Borden, letting the tears and the stories pour out, as an assistant wrote them all down. With those thoughts on paper and others beating in my head, Robert and I worked eight hours a day until Christmas on a script. Robert is what's called a "showrunner," a producer responsible for keeping story and characters on track, and in his quiet, thoughtful way he helped craft a pilot script that soared like the Wright Brothers at Kitty Hawk.

Warner Bros. loved it. Sandy loved it. Only no network was jumping at the chance to sign a supersized Latino for the small screen.

OTHER VOICES, SANDY BULLOCK

Maybe the funniest part of all this is that having never done television, I would just blindly go in, had no problem making calls to the networks, saying, "You've got to go see George's act." And so they would go to, say, the Improv, and we'd separate all the networks at different tables—ABC, CBS, NBC—me playing hostess. I feel like, looking back, had I known then what I know now, would have I been so brave? Probably not.

It was interesting to watch what happened: They all loved his energy, were amazed by the show, but we weren't able to make a deal. They were all like, "We don't know what to do. He's very funny. But there's no place." And I'm thinking, No place? You don't have a place for a really funny show? It didn't occur to me, until George explained later, what they meant.

After all, it had been only thirty years since the debut of *Chico* on network TV. Three long decades of disappointment on both sides of the ledger—Latinos on the outside looking in, studio execs on the inside struggling to find an ethnic show that could cross over and deliver the kind of mainstream numbers that make producing prime-time television worthwhile.

Remember the Courts of Remembrance and the Sanctuary of Light, the final resting place for Freddie Prinze at Forest Lawn? Remember how in times of trouble I said that I would return to pray for inspiration or some kind of divine intervention—for Freddie to reach down and guide my life in a positive direction? Well, the morning before a huge meeting with ABC, I went to see Freddie again.

"Please," I said, "let me have the opportunity to do a show. Let me have an opportunity to fulfill my dream, to connect through TV history, you and me."

Even today I have trouble believing what happened next. I headed home to change, then went to the office of Stu Bloomberg, the head of ABC Entertainment at the time, in a teal-blue building on the back lot of Warner's with all the charm of an insurance office. There was quite a crowd: Bruce, Sandy, Deborah Oppenheimer, another terrific executive producer, a couple of ABC creative people. No sooner had I sat down on a couch when I noticed something, as did Stu.

"Kinda dark in here," he says. "Mind if I open the shades?"

And I'm thinking, *Kind of dark in* my life *right now.*

He walks over to the window and opens the drapes, and from a seated position my eyes carry straight across the road . . . into Forest

Lawn and *directly* into the Courts of Remembrance and Sanctuary of Light. It's like I've channeled my idol. And all I can think of is, *Motherfu—* *Freddie, you heard me, you're with me now . . .*

At which point, Robert and I proceeded to blow Bloomberg away.

"Okay, I like the script, George works in a factory—what else you got?" he said.

We got characters and stories. We leave no fucking stone unturned. That's what *we got.* And before we left we got something else: a four-episode commitment from ABC-TV for a new show.

The *George Lopez* show.

THE LAMP

The one thing that will never change, as long as we're Latinos, is the fact that we never want to get anything repaired. We don't want to hire a repairman.

At any old Mexican woman's house there's always a lamp that's even older than she is. It's been around for like fifty years. No cord. And it's a total fire hazard. Or maybe it does have cord coming out that has a big ball of black tape on it—or a red cord, not even the original cord. You walk by it, you step on the cord, and it sounds like the world's largest hummingbird. And your grandma says, "It makes crinkles. Mijo, please fix it for me."

"What's the matter with it?"

"I don't know, fix it, please. I can't see—my eyes. I'm in the dark, *nombre.*"

So you lean in back behind the couch, but there's no space, because Mexican people push all the furniture up against the walls. You put your hand in, you touch the cord, and it, like, vaporizes your hand. And you look over at your grandmother and she's got this shit-eating grin, trying to hold it in.

"*Lo siento, mijo,* I'm sorry, that's why I didn't do it."

The lamp is important. It's always on. Chicanos don't have an alarm in the house. No code. "Hang on, I need to put my code in because we're going over to Chad and Muffy's. Blue Jay, okay, there you go. Fantastic."

Us? "Hey, man, we're gonna go to Las Vegas, eh. Leave the light on. So that way they think somebody's home." Leave it on, *porque* people, burglars walk by, they go, '*Nombre, mira,* they're up at two o'clock in the morning. Forget it.' *Or we leave the radio on because that way we have audio-visual security.*

And that lamp never has a shade, just a bulb, and you ask where that shade is, and you get, "On the way over, I don't know, I think it's on Van Owen. I drove by, but I couldn't see it."

My grandfather didn't know anything about lamps or lights. So he goes outside and brings in this big halogen light from the garage. "*Mira, mira,*" *he says.* "*It's going to fit.*"

And I told him, "You know, Cuco, I don't think you should be putting—"

"*Mira, shut up, cabrón, you—you worry about your life, and let, mira*"*—he turns it on and you can hear this buzzing noise. Bzzzzz, bzzzzz. The bulb is already about a thousand degrees, that bulb, you don't even want to go near it, when by accident, you're talking, and you lean into it. And you can hear your skin—Aahhhhh!*

"*Mira, the room changed color . . .*"

"*Qué pasó, it turned beige, qué?*"

So now you've got a red-ass dot on your arm. So you go to the barbecue, and your grandmother is like, "Get your ass over here. What did I tell you about tattoos?"

So you mumble something.

"I can't hear you."

"You don't like tattoos."

"I don't like them? I DON'T LIKE THEM? And still you get the tattoo to your arm."

"Huh?"

"*Muy bonito.* You like that. Who's Sylvania? Is she the black girl that works at Home Depot, *cabrón?* Sylvania. Don't tell me she's not black. It says 'Watts' right on your arm. Watts, *pendejo.* Sylvania 75 Watts. I don't know the street, *cabrón,* but I know the town. I'll find her. Seventy-five Watts."

SHOW TIME

FADE IN:

INT GEORGE, SANDY, BRUCE, ASSORTED ABC HEAVY
HITTERS, AND WARNER BROS. PRESIDENT PETER ROTH,
SEATED IN A PLUSH STUDIO CONFERENCE ROOM.

(TIGHT ON GEORGE, LOOKING NERVOUS)

> HEAVY HITTER
> What do you think, George?

(GEORGE HESITATES. UNSURE . . .)

> BRUCE
> We'll do midseason if you put us on Wednesdays. And
> if you put us on after "My Wife and Kids." And move
> Belushi for four weeks.

And that's exactly what happened. The network wanted six episodes,
but I didn't like the idea. I didn't know much about TV, but I was
pretty sure there was a huge learning curve right around the corner.

The timing would be way too tight to write, produce, and shoot six episodes. So we stuck to four.

OTHER VOICES—SANDY BULLOCK

Somehow all the stars aligned in our favor and all of a sudden 'we're being pushed as a midseason replacement, a half-year earlier than we wanted. We've got no writers, no director, no tools whatsoever. It was like ABC said, "Well, we let you have the show, but we're not going to give you any help." I'm like, "Don't you know who I am?"

Take casting, for example. We figured there'd be so much talent—wrong. Because there was no real demand for Latino actors in television, agents didn't take them on as clients. There were some great character actors because those were the roles, but we needed more. We talked about going to Mexico City or the soaps.

We even wanted our crew to have at least an element of Latino blood, and they would tell us, "There's not much use for us. Shows are always starting then stopping in a matter of a couple of months." But I like problems, I like taking chances because the rewards are so much greater.

Nearly three years and fifty-six episodes later, I've learned one key fact: Whether it's funny, unfunny, or somewhere in between, doing a network television situation comedy, aka a sitcom, is a five- or six-day-a-week *process*. Some weeks it feels like five years.

Now, the process is rather pleasant if you're only occasionally called out of your dressing room or air-conditioned Star Wagon to recite a line or two and then return to the trappings of network TV. But if you're involved in every single aspect of the show, if your *name* is on it, you do what I do, which on any given week goes something like this:

Monday: A production meeting followed by a time-honored tradition in television known as the Table Read. Whereby the cast and every major person connected to the show—executives, producers, writers—sit in comfy clothes around tables turned into a rectangle and read literally every line of the script, getting a feel for the flow of the story. In the hands of former actor turned director Joe Regalbuto, who starred on the hysterical *Murphy Brown,* the table read resembles something of a pep rally. He welcomes the cast back to the show, and everyone claps, and then Joe introduces the week's guest stars, and everyone claps, and then we read the script out loud and everyone laughs. It's a feel-good kind of hour, a much-needed way to recharge our batteries. Then we rehearse for the rest of the day. If the script needs it, I'll go back to the writer's room and grind until nine or ten.

Tuesday: Rehearse for three hours in the morning and two more in the afternoon before staging what's called a network/studio run-through. Another time-honored drill where network and show execs, writers, agents, lucky friends and family watch the show in essentially real time before the execs offer "notes" designed to improve the product. After that, most often, another night until seven or eight sharpening scenes and lines with the writers.

Wednesday: Camera blocking followed by five more hours of rehearsal. During downtime, in the quiet of my dressing room, I run lines with my acting and dialogue coaches, on my way to memorizing scripts that run forty pages or more.

Thursday: Show Day. From 10:30 to 3:30 about 80 percent of the script is shot on a closed set. Around 5:00 P.M.

there's hair, makeup, and wardrobe, followed by final notes and script revision. At 5:25 the cast is introduced to a live audience and at 5:30 we hit the stage running. About 80 percent of what's shot here makes air. Three and a half hours of shooting for twenty-two minutes of television.

In the beginning I had no idea what I was in for, no idea about the subtleties of acting—how to walk and talk, hit a mark, play to a camera or even stand in the right light. It was like learning a new language while living in a foreign country: There's no time to assimilate. They throw you in, and you either sink or swim.

Take walking and talking. Sounds easy, right? But try it while moving across a crowded kitchen while conveying anger or hurt. Knowing you've got four steps to reach your main camera and the most flattering light. In stand-up, your natural instinct is to play it big, to exaggerate hand and facial gestures. In television, it's just the opposite. Early on, one of the blunt, tough notes I got from an ABC exec was to stop "bugging out" my eyes at every surprise, and he was right.

John Pasquin, who directed *Home Improvement* and many memorable episodes of *Roseanne,* is one of those whom I credit with helping me understand the *art* of television. In rehearsal, he's constantly tweaking lines, sharpening timing, massaging scenes, all in a gentle manner. It's the pauses and hesitations that connect emotionally with the people at home. It's fascinating to see storytelling of another stripe come to life in the hands of someone like John. He knows exactly how families, at least our family, are supposed to sound.

Thanks to John, Sandy, Bruce, one of my *vatos of golf,* producer Frank Pace, and so many other pros, I've learned that the *art* is letting little lines and looks build to big moments. That's what you're always playing to—the moments.

We busted our ass on those first four episodes, because for me there was no second chance. I had to hit the jackpot in those first four pulls or go the way of every other Latino-based sitcom since 1974. You see, there's a reason we Latinos have such great rhythm. For us, the dance is far more complex: We have been dancing our entire life, often to another man's beat, and, yes, while

we make much more of our own music now, for Latinos in television it's different. Making people laugh is not enough. Despite the fact there are thirty-nine *million* and counting of us, and advertisers, publishers, and marketers beating a path to our doors, we still scare people—the powerful people—in Hollywood. They still see us as the help—raising their kids, cutting their grass, cooking their food—not as friends or equals. It's what they see, and not what they know.

I was out to change that view.

One television writer so eloquently noted that all I had to do was "appeal to the widest possible audience while convincing viewers his show isn't ethnically or culturally exclusive while making Latino viewers feel special and understood."

Yeah, all in a week's work.

FADE IN:

INT. HBO STUDIOS, 120A EAST 23RD STREET, NEW YORK CITY

(ON THE SET OF "ON THE RECORD" WITH HOST BOB COSTAS. BOB AND GEORGE, ALONE, TALKING)

BOB
How true can you be to presenting whatever your vision is of life—your life, or some slice of Mexican-American culture. But at the same time the show needs to be a mainstream hit, so there's got to be something that appeals to a broader audience—so how do you walk that line?

GEORGE
We let what we look like do the speaking
for all that other stuff. We just try to
be people, general regular people.
Except we've got great tans.

BOB
As you said, I don't want to be so much a Mexican
as a human being, a human being who is Mexican.
Which may seem like a simple concept—

GEORGE
It's the toughest thing to do. I got a call from an
executive who says to me, "George, there's nothing
in the kitchen that tells anybody that a Mexican
family lives there." They wanted to put in a tortilla
maker. I don't even know what that is. My
grandmother was my tortilla maker. So I told them,
"What about the Mexicans in the kitchen?"

In the first show we spoke exactly one word of Spanish.

In the past when Latinos got mad on television, it turned into
Telemundo: *como es pendejo, por favor, no, señor.* That wasn't going to
happen here. Sure, we tossed in a *chichi* or two for good measure, but
we wanted to go easy; I wanted the show to stand on its heart and
humor. I wasn't interested in playing to one coalition or another. We
were trying to hit the ball right up the middle.

I found my inspiration, strangely enough, not in baseball but
football, Notre Dame football, to be exact. There's a sign above the
door leading the Fighting Irish onto the field that reads, "Play Like a
Champion Today." That was my goal: to be the champions of our

time slot, then of a night, then of the entire network. To that end we signed ourselves a damn good team.

Constance Marie (my wife, Angie) is a dark-haired beauty with big brown eyes. She and I go back about ten years to the days I was hustling a *Honeymooners* kind of thing. The first time we met, we ended up doing improv for about twenty minutes, and it was amazing. We didn't interact much again until it was time to cast my wife. Ann and Mary Buck, a major casting director, fought for Constance and she won the part. She's had knocks and struggles of her own and I respect her journey and how she is not only finding her way but flourishing as well.

Belita Moreno (my mother, Benny) is a terrific actress who is actually a lot younger than she looks (she *demanded* I include that) and appears to have been channeling my grandmother for several years now. She gets a lot of laughs in the show and earns every one of them because she is, without question, the most thorough actor of us all. If we have a purse on the show Belita wants to know where it's from, how it was made, what kind of thread was used. I'm, like, Belita, it's a *purse,* but that's her method and it works.

I also have great respect for Masiela Lusha (my daughter, Carmen) and Luis Garcia (my son, Max). They've both come a long way, so far their heads could be as big as mine—*oh, my God*—but instead they're two of the brightest, most talented, level-headed kids I know. Along with Valente Rodriguez (my best friend, Ernie), who steals just about every scene he's in, we're all blazing trails.

Thus every time I run to the stage on show night I pray for a little luck of the Irish. Reminding myself to play like a champion while telling myself, "This is number one . . . number two . . . number three."

We debuted March 27, 2002. The first four shows were rocky, to say the least, works in progress with ten new writers, a fresh cast, and four

different directors. Hit shows all enjoy a certain rhythm, a vision, and a voice and early on, we struggled to find ours, but thankfully we found enough of an audience to merit a shot on the fall schedule. It didn't hurt when a certain A-list actress with a heart of gold stepped up and offered to guest-star for four weeks during November sweeps as "Accident Amy," a klutzy coworker who, in Sandy's words, was "an enthusiastic person with a slight depth-perception problem."

FADE IN. SUPERIMPOSE DATE (AUGUST 2001)

GEORGE, IN A TOWN CAR, DEPARTING HOUSTON AIRPORT HEADED FOR A COMEDY GIG, WHEN CELL PHONE RINGS.

SFX: PHONE RING

> GEORGE
> Hello.

HELFORD IN HIS OFFICE AT WARNER BROS.
> BRUCE
> Are you sitting down?

> GEORGE
> Yeah.

> BRUCE
> Congratulations. ABC just decided to go beyond the four and give us a thirteen-week commitment. (Pause) You got your show.

GEORGE, STUNNED, STARES OUT THE WINDOW, TEARS COMING TO HIS EYES.

GEORGE
Wow. (Pause) Really, Bruce?

BRUCE
You should be really happy, man. Enjoy
the day.

GEORGE CLICKS OFF CELL PHONE AND LOOKS AT THE
ONLY OTHER PERSON IN THE CAR, HIS DRIVER, STARING
BACK NOW THROUGH THE REARVIEW MIRROR.

GEORGE
Hey, man, I just got a show on ABC.

DRIVER OFFERS NO RESPONSE, BUT BEFORE TURNING HIS
EYES BACK TO THE ROAD GIVES GEORGE A "YEAH, SURE,
THAT'LL WORK . . ." KIND OF LOOK AS WE:

FADE OUT.

We got a coveted slot—Wednesdays at eight-thirty, behind Damon Wayans's *My Wife and Kids,* beginning the first week in October. By the last week we were the talk of the town. The most-watched program in our time period, we were drawing twelve million or more viewers a week, the vast majority of whom were *not* Hispanic. Major newspapers trumpeted our growing appeal. *People* put us "in the spotlight." Suddenly, that single blade of grass fighting to break through that crack in the sidewalk was cracking through. *The first successful Latino sitcom on network TV since* Chico and the Man.

ABC execs saw the numbers and started calling the show "a new voice" and a "fresh take" on family comedy. And thanks to scripts like "Who's Your Daddy," "Token of Unappreciation," "Profiles in

Courage," and "Guess Who's Coming to Dinner," we kept doing what Sandy calls "pushing the edge"— tackling subjects ranging from racial stereotyping to the search for my long-lost dad. We caught America's eye—and held it—while drawing praise from the notoriously difficult-to-please Latino community.

I barely slept. I wanted to smash every Latino stereotype and raise the bar for every Anglo writer, producer, and executive out there who thinks that because his housekeeper is doing such a great job with *Cole,* he can write a show that Latinos are going to find interesting. We were proof that an ensemble cast, no matter the creed or color, can mine "this rich vein of gloom," as *The New York Times* called it, and live to laugh about it.

Like "This Old Casa," a show written by the incisive Rick Nyholm that we shot in November 2002. In yet another vain attempt to extract even a dollop of praise from my grandmother, I completely redo her bathroom, a perfect example of not only mining that vein but playing to the moments.

(INDICATING THE BATHROOM)

GEORGE
Do you know why I did all this? To get you to say "thank you." Then I realized there's a lot of things I never thanked you for.

(WITH DIFFICULTY)
I know how hard it was raising me alone. Thank you for your sacrifices, thank you for taking care of me when I was sick, thank you for being both my mom and dad. Thank you for all the things I don't even know you did for me.

(THEN)
Now, do you have anything to say to me?

BENNY
It's about freakin' time.

GEORGE
You're really not getting this, Mom. You
see, I opened up, I feel good about it.
Now it's your turn to open up.

BENNY
Okay. But this is gonna be hard for me . . . I like
movies where dogs can talk.

GEORGE
What I'm looking for, Mom, is two little words. Three
if you say it "blank blank, George." Or you could say
it, "George, blank, blank." Hey, I'll even make it
easier for you—in Spanish it's just one word.

BENNY
Adios.

And deeper into Act Two, Scene E, come the words you long to
hear . . . just as I'm ready to destroy the bathroom.

BENNY
Thank you for the damn toilet seat! There. You
happy? Is that what you wanted?

GEORGE
Yes. Was that so hard?

BENNY
Yeah. I don't have a lot of practice doing this. Who
do I thank for having to drop out of school at
fifteen to work in a factory? Who do I thank for

getting me pregnant at sixteen? Who do I thank for feeling sixty-eight when I was twenty-five? But thank God I know who to thank for getting me a cushioned toilet seat.

(GEORGE CROSSES TO HER. THERE'S A BEAT. BENNY CROSSES OVER TO THE TUB AND SITS ON THE EDGE. THERE'S A BEAT)

GEORGE
I love you, Mom.

BENNY
Thank you.

(AFTER A BEAT)

GEORGE
You just opened up.

BENNY
No, I didn't.

GEORGE
Yeah, you did.

BENNY
No, I didn't.

GEORGE
I'm pretty sure you did.

BENNY
What do you know? You put the soap dish too far away from the shower head.

GEORGE
That's 'cause it's an ashtray.

BENNY
Really? That's so nice. You know what? You're a pretty good son.

GEORGE
Thank you.

BENNY
You give it up way too easy.

(AS THEY EXIT, WE:)

FADE OUT.

It was due to such moments that critics from *The New York Times* to the *Los Angeles Times* to *The Wall Street Journal* began to take notice. Comedies like ours, said *The New York Times,* finally "reflect the fluid, fragmented reality of the modern American house."

I liked that.

I liked our ratings even more. We moved into the top twenty-five shows. We were playing in Peoria.

Suddenly, one month into a thirteen-week commitment, I was being called the "savior" of ABC Wednesdays. About to receive even bigger backing from the network.

FADE IN:

INT. GEORGE'S DRESSING ROOM AT WARNER BROS. ASSORTED PHOTOGRAPHS. SHRINE TO PRINZE AND PRYOR. GEORGE WORKING ON HIS LAPTOP

SFX: KNOCK ON DOOR

> GEORGE
> Come in.

(BRUCE HELFORD ENTERS)

> BRUCE
> I just want to tell you what's going to happen. You're going to get a lot of power, ultimate power. You're going to have more power than me. Than Warner Bros. Than ABC because they're going to want to make you happy. So you must make sure you don't abuse that power. Make sure you're kind to the writers and kind to the crew and kind to the cast. Some people have made mistakes, and it's important you remain pure and true.

SFX: PHONE RINGS

> GEORGE
> Hello.

(TIGHT ON GEORGE. TALKING ON THE PHONE)

CUT TO INT. OFFICE OF ABC ENTERTAINMENT CHIEF SUSAN LYNE

SUSAN
George, I just wanted to tell you we've picked up the show for the back nine.

CUT TO: (TIGHT ON GEORGE, TEARS IN HIS EYES AS HE HANGS UP.)

When I got back to the set I called the entire cast and crew together, barely able to contain my emotions. The "back nine" meant ABC was commiting to an entire season—twenty-two episodes.

Warner Bros. President Peter Roth was at my side and spoke first. "The truth of the matter is," he began, "what makes this so special, so rewarding, so extraordinary, is this is the first Latino family sitcom that has been as successful as this one—you guys have made history—and that is something you should be very, very proud of. Secondly, from those of us who sit in ivory towers and watch, the shows are so beautifully crafted, they're about *something,* the quality of the execution is as good as I've seen and is reflected in the audience that is there for you. And what is happening is, you guys are holding the audience of the No. 1 rated sitcom on all of ABC. It's an amazing accomplishment. Congratulations."

Now it was time for Teary Guy.

"Everybody has been with the show—from the broadcast assistants to the writer's assistants to everybody in the office to the delivery guy with all the tattoos—everybody that comes to work to make *George Lopez,* the show, a success, George Lopez, me, I just want to tell each and every one of you, I love you so much, and thank you, thank you, for making my dream."

Since our country can't seem to get enough of gambling, if you consider the economics of network TV one giant slot machine, you'll get why such a commitment by Warners means so much.

Every year studios take enormous gambles on shows. For example, Warner Bros. Television bankrolls about five new half-hour comedies a year at an average of thirteen episodes per show. That's sixty-five episodes at about $250,000 to $300,000 per show. For the mathematically impaired, that equals about $20 million dropped into the comedy slot alone every season.

Now pull the handle five times. Place a bet, a huge bet on each of those new comedies, and that's the risk Warner's taking. The reward—and it's a big one—comes if one or two of those pulls hit the fucking jackpot: the magic eighty-eight episode syndication mark that spells riches all around. The rest are just one long line of mixed fruit.

How big is syndication? This big: *Friends* took in about $1 *billion* in first-time syndication; *Who's the Boss,* with Tony Danza, raked in some $600 million the first time around. The point: If your show syndicates, and you own a nice piece of it, you win.

Now don't laugh when I say this, but it's not about the money to me. (Okay, you can laugh a little.) I don't sit around and throw it on the bed, dreaming about how I'll never have to work again. After we got renewed for a third season in 2002–2003—twenty-two more episodes—all I could think about was the fourth year, then the fifth, then the sixth, then the seventh . . . because I've worked too fucking hard to let go now. I tell actors on my show that none of them and their insecurities or demands or their unprofessionalism is going to affect me. I'll write them out of my fuckin' show. That's the way it is, man. No one is going to stand between me and my show. I know I'm not getting a second chance.

"You don't *understand,*" Bruce once told an actor who had come in unprepared. "This is his *life.* So when you disrespect the show, you're fucking with his life. You don't know how deep this dude is devoted to the show."

I spoke about the "ghosts" of comedy a while ago. Well, at Warner Bros. Television, and especially our home, Sound Stage 4, the influences seem more visible and concrete. *42nd Street* was the first film shot here, in 1933, followed, in part, by *Casablanca* in '43, *My Fair Lady* ('64), *All the President's Men* ('76) and *Blade Runner* ('82).

Moreover, Clint Eastwood's Malpaso Productions is housed in Bungalow 16 across our little street; George Clooney and director Steven Soderbergh share Bungalow 15 next door. *ER* shoots in a cavernous sound stage not one hundred yards away from my dressing room; Candice Bergen and the cast of *Murphy Brown* once used Stage 4 for their stellar show.

Everywhere I look I'm surrounded by people devoted to the craft. And I just don't mean Clint or George but also carpenters, painters, hair and makeup people, set designers, many of whom depend on me to feed their families.

Believe it or not, the budget for our 2003–2004 season was more than $30 million. At any given time, more than 125 people, including forty full-timers, work the show. So when I talk about a "family," that's exactly what we've got going here, and I take my role as the head of it very seriously. I said from the start I wanted to produce a situation that was good for the *show*, for the entire *family*. It wasn't about showcasing my talent but creating an environment, a family dynamic, that would allow others to flourish as well.

FADE IN:

EXT. 19TH HOLE, UPSCALE GOLF COURSE—AFTERNOON
GEORGE, JOHNNY THE GUARD, VERN, AND BARRY FROM
CRAFT SERVICES

(WIDE ON THE GROUP REVEALING CHARITY
RAFFLE FOR THE DISNEY BOYS AND GIRLS
CLUB, HOSTED BY GEORGE)

GEORGE
What's my bid for this beautiful Big
Bertha, whose head looks about as the size of mine.

CROWD VOICE
Seventy-five dollars.

GEORGE
One twenty-five.

(LOOKING AROUND)
Going once, twice, sold . . . to me.

(LATER, GEORGE HANGING AT THE BAR WITH GUYS FROM
THE SHOW. THERE ARE TEARS IN VERN'S EYES)

VERN
I never had anybody do that for me.

GEORGE
C'mon Vern.

VERN
No, man. I'm going through some hard times. I just
want to thank you.

GEORGE
That's how you do it, Vern.

Yes, sometimes being the head of a family means shelling out six hundred for a foursome and hanging with Johnny the guard, Valente's stand-in, and Barry from Craft Services. Or taking a break on a very long day and shooting the breeze with the "laughers," the motley crew that shows up on Wednesday for free food and coffee in exchange for sitting patiently for hours and laughing on cue.

People tell me, "George, nobody talks to the laughers."

Well, I do.

OTHER VOICES—SANDY BULLOCK

How has the show affected me? From a producing standpoint, it's such a great ego boost to find that dark horse, to find the most incredible comedic athlete and see him run like this, to see things in papers like, "TV has a fresh new face."

What did it do for me personally? I had hit a huge burnout stage and I wasn't crazy about being in the business anymore. I still wanted to be part of the creative process, but I didn't want to be in front of the camera, to carry all that responsibility. But after watching George and Constance and Belita, the entire cast, really, I'm motivated by them as actors, seeing the audience react, their sense of pride; it has inspired me creatively. With all the success they haven't forgotten how they got there: Like George, every time he comes out before the show, he grabs the mike and does a little of his comedy thing, then always, always, always brings up someone from the crew, or a guy who's been a buddy for fifteen years and happens to be in the audience.

Unlike most actors, George is so appreciative, so vulnerable, and it means all the more to me knowing I didn't create a monster. He's an amazing actor and comic, but he's an even more amazing human being. He's got something in him, this invincibility, no,

that's not a good word, this resilience, *because he had to learn to survive at such an early age in ways no child should ever have to learn. Because of that he's braver than most other actors—the crew feels it, the cast feels it, Bruce feels it, we all feel it.*

So who's crying now?

Certainly those who whispered we'd strike out early on four pitches. The count's in our favor now. Three years ago we were just one of twenty. Now we're one of only seven shows considered strong enough to lead a night. In 2002 I sat by myself at an ABC function for advertisers and took the stage behind Damon Wayans and Tisha Campbell. This year at the same kind of function, I brought the whole cast and we walked out at Radio City Music Hall leading the Friday night lineup. Even if I get canceled tomorrow, that's one of the things I can take with me.

I honestly don't believe a lot of what's happening in my life right now. It's moving so fast: a featured role in the powerful, critically acclaimed movie *Real Women Have Curves;* a coveted invitation from Clint Eastwood to play the AT&T at Pebble Beach; a Parents Television Council "Seal of Approval" award; a major Showtime concert special; a Grammy nomination for my *Team Leader* CD. Late last year I even hosted the Greatest TV Moments of 2003 for *TV Guide.*

My greatest moment? One nominee would certainly be when, earlier this year, Disney ordered six more episodes of the show, upping our season total to a twenty-eight and three-year total to fifty-six.

Another nominee occurred a couple months earlier. As you know, for the longest time a certain groundbreaking group has been my musical savior, and as a tribute I asked the guys from WAR to come on the set and to play "Low Rider" to close our first full year's season finale. Originally, the script called for the entire cast to dance. But my friend Frank Pace, who has helped produce the likes of *Sud-*

denly Susan and *Head of the Class,* offered an emotional rewrite.

"Don't let the whole cast dance," he said. "It ought to be about you, your struggle, your journey. Take the moment, man."

So I did, pretending to play drums with the band. And what a moment it was.

But thinking back, the winner probably arrived last December. My greatest TV moment starting out on a back lot at Warner's on one of those indescribable Southern California mornings. The crew setting up a scene for our Christmas week show. The writers, coming off a late-night jag, racing around in an impromptu game of soccer. And me, in costume, looking on, smoking a Cuban.

Puffing away I felt like a proud *papi.* The writers finally lost steam and wrapped up their game. One by one, they peeled the sweat-stained T-shirts off their backs. Then they all proudly pulled on new shirts emblazoned with the name of our show across the front—my name.

Having never celebrated much of anything, I stood, dressed as ol' St. Nick, thinking, *Merry Christmas, Santa, for a gift, a moment, that keeps on giving.*

NOW'S THE TIME

Mexicans are always late. You want to piss somebody off, be early.

Anglos, they're late and what you get is this:

"Oh, my God, I'm sooo sorry. I have a note from the highway patrolmen. There was a jackknifed big rig. I'm sooo sorry."

Us? We show up later than late and everyone's mad. "Hey, wassup? How come everyone's mad? You're mad at me, fuck, I just got here . . . How come I'm late? I thought you were going to be late, that's why I'm late."

Why are we always so late? Not sure. Probably because we think it takes fifteen minutes to get anywhere.

"Where you going? Bakersfield . . . about fifteen minutes. Get to the Grapevine in about eight minutes. You don't need gas, you just get to the top, put it in neutral, and coast all the way down . . ."

Another reason we're always late is that none of the clocks work in our house. They all need batteries.

"What kind of batteries, Grandma?"

"I don't know, the ah-ah. I need the ah-ah. Two ah-ahs for the little Mickey Mouse clock, and four ahhhhhs for my little flashlight. So I can see my way . . ."

The TV was our clock. "Grandma," I would say, "what time do you take your medicine?"

"Cuando la Judge Judy, *I take my pill. But one day I couldn't find, mira."*

"The remote control?"

"The pliers! I couldn't find the pliers. To change the TV. Somebody took the pincas, I don't know where they went. Whoever used the oven didn't put them back on the TV."

Yeah, you could be playing out in the yard, all happy, and suddenly you'd hear, "Jorge!"

"What?"

"Put on Channel Five."

The next thing you know you're standing next to the tube. Holding the pliers.

"Don't move. Stand right there. Matlock is coming on. Stand right here. Put that face away. Put the face—put the face away."

The microwave was our other clock.

"Cabrón, go in the kitchen and see what time it is."

So you wander in, look at the number without thinking, and yell out, "Ah, fourteen."

"Cabrón, read it!"

"I already did—I told you it's fourteen."

"Cabrón, push Clear! Idiota, push Clear!"

SUMMER FUN

We stopped filming the second season of the show in April 2003, and everyone said, George, you look tired. Make sure you get some rest. Get a massage. Take some multivitamins. Get more sleep, some facials.

You know what I said? Fuck that, I'm going to Abilene . . .

And Austin . . . Albuquerque . . . Denver . . . Amarillo, Laredo, San Angelo, El Paso . . . and a half-dozen other cities.

For me fun in the sun isn't lying on the beach for two or three months or flying to Hawaii for that "much needed" vacation. For me summer fun means hitting the road to hone my act and close the gap. More than anything, my annual summer concert tour—and weekend gigs around the state—*ground* me, helping me connect as much as possible with people who watch my show, buy my CDs, and write hundreds of e-mails like this to me at georgelopez.com:

> Finally, someone us Chicanos can relate to. Love your comedy! We will be at the first of two shows tonight in Phoenix. Can't wait.

And this:

> I would like to congratulate you on your success as a Hispanic comedian. I watched you first when you came

on the *Qué Locos* show, then my best friend
played your CD *Right Now Right Now* which
was very hilarious. Of course, I had to share it
with my coworkers at Home Depot, especially
the Holmes Depot part. I would love to see you
in person. Maybe when you come to San
Diego I will have a chance to see you

And this:

> George Lopez is the meaning of Chicano. George,
> you are the one who put prime-time television in the
> home of many Mexicans with your show. I am an aspiring
> comedian and really don't know how to get started. I look
> to guys like you to open doors for young Chicanos like
> me. Hopefully, I will meet you someday and crack you up.

And this:

> It's great to see you are a positive activist for the
> Hispanic community. We need more like you. Keep up
> the excellent work and do not give up stand-up comedy. I
> enjoy watching your concerts!

That is why I tour, why I still do stand-up. Yeah, make no mistake, the money is great—even more so now that I know I don't need
it to feed my family. But the real rush for me has always been breaking
down walls. And not just the one tagged "Latino Comics Can't
Draw" (three straight nights of 6,500 people at the Universal Amphitheatre near Los Angeles last October shattered that myth) but also
the barrier between you and me. Like I said in the beginning, I'm as
real and tragic as anyone out there. I'm not embarrassed by that statement anymore; instead, I draw strength from it. In concerts, that
strength is amplified—transcending the tiny box called television in a
way that's far more personal and powerful. Yeah, I love making people

laugh. But I like making them feel *stronger and empowered* just as much.

So with that in mind we struck out on a "Team Leader" tour: fifteen sold-out cities in sixteen days, rolling along in a Big Red bus, Big Charlie from Nashville at the wheel, with Ron and the hilarious Lowell "Man Overboard" Sanders, my good friend and longtime opening act, along for the ride. We started out at the KIVA Auditorium in Albuquerque the first week of June before winding our way into Colorado for a couple of concerts followed by a twelve-day stretch deep in the heart of Texas.

In its purest form, classic stand-up is comparable to a classic car. Any comic worth a shit can step onstage and take an audience for a ten-minute ride. But what about twenty? Or thirty? Or sixty? Or one hundred and ten minutes, where the white dot on my diver's watch is set for every major show?

When you're in the gifted hands of a Prinze, Pryor, Rock, Williams, Newhart, Foxx, or Buttons—to name but a few—that time simply flies. You're seated in the back of a washed, polished and shined-to-perfection automobile, featuring great lines and styling, no wasted motion or ill-timed stops and starts. Nothing but pure driving—or listening—pleasure.

Our first show in New Mexico proved more Ford than Ferrari. By the second night, in Greeley, Colorado, I felt my motor humming but quickly hit a rather large bump in the road in Abilene: much to my surprise Abilene turned out to be a rock-ribbed conservative and deeply religious Christian community.

A telltale sign of just how conservative came courtesy of Donnie, the groundskeeper at the local golf course. Before Lowell and I teed off the following morning, there was Donnie drawling, "I'm going to see yawl too-night. It ain't going to be pro-fane, is it?" Then he said, "Well, I don't care if it is."

Then I thought: he wouldn't have asked if pro-fanity didn't bother him. Which got me thinking about the girl at the hotel who had driven us to the course: she said she was coming with her parents.

Five years earlier I never would have picked up on those signs. And if I did get an inkling that the crowd wouldn't have taken kindly to some four-letter specials, I'd have been stumped onstage. Not now. These days, I've discovered, I can deliver a PG-13 show—the clean-cut version of a dysfunctional life—without sacrificing a whole lot of laughs. It's that jazz comedy I talked about: sometimes you play it smoky in clubs down in Greenwich Village where anything goes and sometimes you play it straight in the Civic Center in Abilene. It's all art.

And it worked. Every last bit. It was *tight*. I did an hour and thirty-five minutes in Abilene driving right past that little white dot on my watch and never looked back.

After the Abilene show, Charlie didn't get us cruising into Austin until nearly three in the morning. I spent most of the day Friday hanging out in the Presidential Suite at the Four Seasons, watching golf on TV. Six years earlier I was sweating it out in a local Residence Inn, knowing I'd face a near-empty room at the Capital City Comedy Club that night. On this night I knew 2,200 people would pack the Paramount Theatre, most of the crowd dressed to the nines, showing how this vibrant, high-tech city has boomed into an increasingly upscale Latino stronghold.

Maybe a bit *too* vibrant because before I stepped on the stage for the eight P.M. show, Lowell got treated to a case of clucking chickens. When I heard three or four groups were taking turns mouthing off and disrupting his act I got pissed. So pissed, I raced backstage in my socks to tell Robin Tate, our ace show promoter, that 1,100 people had come to see this show and Lowell Sanders is an integral part of it. And these yahoos had two options: to shut the fuck up or get the fuck out.

I know how to handle a rowdy crowd now, and the thing I've

learned is: don't let it start. You heckle me and you immediately see the *street George*. I get like my grandmother—*mean*. Last November, for example, I had a real problem with a crowd in San Diego and I just stopped the show. I'd come into the night on edge to begin with—still in shock over the sudden death of my good friend and ABC colleague John Ritter; still unclear whether to talk about a week of horrific wildfires still raging all over San Diego County; still unsettled by the war in Iraq. I decided not to make direct reference to the fires or the troops, instead hanging a large American flag behind me onstage. That was my statement. Then in the second show I started talking about attending Dodger games with my grandfather, and some beer-fueled Padres fans in the audience piped up and began to boo.

I just stopped. I couldn't believe what I was hearing.

"Listen," I said. "I came down here to see *you*. Not the other way around. Ten million people a week watch my show and you *boo* me. We've got soldiers dying in Iraq and you *boo me. Fuck you,* I'll leave this fucking stage right now."

Well, that did it. People cheered. And before the night was over, San Diego proved to be an awesome crowd and memorable show.

A lot of that attitude comes from one man. He wouldn't take shit from anybody. My stage presence draws heavily from Richard Pryor in other ways as well—very spare, just a microphone, a stand, a table stocked with a few towels and bottles of water, and a high-backed chair. During the course of a concert that microphone stand will serve as a lamp, a kid, a dance partner, my uncle Rudy, and about ten other things. In addition, the physicality of my comedy—plus the voices, the glances up to the balcony to draw that audience in—are effectively, homage to Pryor, the direct result of thousands of hours of studying the genius of King Richard.

Much as I always wanted to meet Freddie, I yearned to meet Richard, and in the late nineties, I finally got my chance during a Comedy Store award party.

Richard, who has long suffered from MS, was in a wheelchair,

dressed in a tux, with a nurse tending his needs. I walked up to the chair.

"Can he hear me?" I asked his nurse.

"Oh yeah," she said.

So I leaned down and whispered in Richard's ear: *"I want to thank you, man, for giving me a life."*

He started to shake and his eyes got all watery.

So did mine.

I know Richard a lot better now thanks to his wife, Jennifer. I recently gave him an XM Radio as a present, and he listens to it all the time. Jennifer replied in kind one day, sending me a vintage pair of 1984 Nikes with "Richard" embossed on the back of the left heel and "Pryor" on the right. They are in a protective case in my dressing room today, along with Jennifer's card:

GEORGE, SO YOU CAN FOLLOW IN
RICHARD'S FOOTSTEPS.

Which, on February 21, 2004, is exactly what I did.

It had been twenty-five years since Richard stalked the stage of the Terrace Theatre in Long Beach and threw me that lifeline when I was drowning in self-pity and doubt. Now, as part of a Showtime special and eventual DVD, I would perform on the same stage as Pryor, offering what I hoped would be my most personal tribute yet. Two shows—both taped, 3,500 fans times two—was the plan.

On air the concert will open just as Richard's did a quarter century ago. A limo pulls up to the theater, I step out, notebook in hand, walk up the steps, and the next thing you know—cut—you see me onstage. The only difference this time was the bouquet of flowers gracing a table. Earlier in the day they'd arrived at the house with this beautiful handwritten note:

Wish we could have been there but as you know Richard haunts that theatre. He and I are there in spirit. Have an awesome show. Love, Jennifer and Richard Pryor.

Well, let me tell you, folks. If you were there, you saw it. Dressed in a clean, baggy chocolate-brown suit and leather shoes, I *killed*.

You know, we're always bragging about bad shit that happens in our life. That's how starved we are for attention, we brag about the BAD shit. Like the guy says, "Tell 'em about the time you got electrocuted. Tell 'em, man."

"Hey, my feet were wet, man, and I plugged the thing in . . . I got up, eh, 'cause that's the way I am, and I felt the 'lectric going through me, but something in my mind told my hands . . . 'cause I was holding a beer, eh, and I didn't drop one drop."

By the time the *'lectic* was done flowing through me, there wasn't an ounce of energy to give; I left it all out there. The next morning I swear I felt like I'd gone ten rounds with Roberto Duran in his prime—bruised hand, finger, knot on elbow, sore hip—from all the physical comedy. But it was worth every ounce of pain. Old stuff, new stuff, no holds barred—there was nothing left. Nothing but thanking Ann for her love and support and bringing Sandy onstage to take a bow.

Back in Austin, Sandy was at the second show. She lives in the city and came back to my dressing room afterward along with filmmaker Robert Rodriguez and his lovely wife, Elizabeth Avellán.

"Great show," said Robert. "Killer."

He would know. His gun-slinging, guitar-toting hero El Mariachi, tore up the screen leading to the *Spy Kids* franchise and, most recently, *Once Upon a Time in Mexico*, starring Antonio Banderas, Salma Hayek, and Johnny Depp. To me, Robert is another shining example

of Chicano power and pride. In the dressing room that night he regaled me with tales of how hard he had to scrape and work to fund his first film. Today, at his state-of-the-art production studio near Austin, he writes, directs, shoots, and scores his flicks far away from the Hollywood crowd.

In many ways San Antonio and I had grown up together. I've played the city at least twenty times over the years—mostly dates at the half-full River Center Comedy Club—but this time it was different, the bustling success of the nation's seventh largest city and one of the largest Mexican-American communities, mirroring my own. It was the only major city in the country where *American Idol* was not number one in its time slot that season; one city where I beat it. Not by a hair or a whisker—but two full ratings points.

That Saturday before Father's Day 2003, I put up some more impressive numbers. We set a theater record, packing all three shows, nearly 7,000 total seats, including a matinee. That's me and San Antonio.

I won't kid you. I was worried about that matinee crowd. I figured at three P.M. because of the success of the TV show, I'd be looking at a lot of mothers, fathers, children, and grandparents, and I was right. It looked like the ten A.M. service at First Baptist Church. So what? I've laughed myself silly a time or two in church so I took out a bit about—how should I say?—eating at the Y, toned down the four-letter words, and tuned up one of my new favorites . . . Country Guy.

"You know, we all know these Country Guys. They're all over Texas . . . you know the one. Big hat. Boots. Weather-beaten face. Belt buckle holding up a stomach well into its last trimester. Call Latinos Nachos.

"The country guy is sitting in a diner, having breakfast, with his back to a bunch of Nachos laughing and talking fast in Spanish.

"So the Country Guy goes, 'Well, there they go, just *habla, habla, habla.' Getting all upset. His friends telling him to quiet down. 'I don't care,' he says, 'I'll tell 'em how I feel . . . '*

"So he turns around and says, 'Why can't yawl learn *to speak* rightly!' "

By the time I stepped onstage for the eight P.M. show I was feeling rather *rightly* myself—in total control from the get-go. The crowd was wild, yowling from the second I came on, and I played it to perfection, riffing, embellishing—allowing the swells to rise and die away . . . waiting for just the right moment to build the wave again before delivering two, three sometimes, shots to the G. Lo spot. *Memmer? . . . U Memmer!* . . . I left pauses where I wouldn't dare before—just looking out and waiting, maybe adding a hand gesture or two, a painter offering a dab or two of color to his canvas—adjusting on the fly, talking from one side of the brain, figuring out how to end the joke with the other side. With about ten minutes left I'm thinking what haven't I done, what kind of finish do I want? That's when it becomes so damn addictive—being in utter control of a moment, not a damn degree of separation between you and your audience.

So I opt for this ending, perfect for the state:

"*You know how Mexican restaurants always have 'border' in them— Border Grill, Border Café, Taco Bell's Run for the Border. You know, you wouldn't do that to black people. Like Kunta's Kitchen. Or Shackles. They don't do it to white people. You don't see things like the Honky Grill . . . or the Cracker Barrel . . . oh, never mind.*"

Finally, at half past midnight, near the end of my third and final Saturday show and four and a half hours of entertaining, I sat slumped in the black high-backed chair, spread my feet, and let the love flow. It's not even a roar now—more like an uproar. A wall of sound that started in the upper reaches of the balcony, gathered force only to ric-

ochet off the stage, off my $1,500 suit, then up across my face and skin, before finally sinking deep into my heart. It stayed right there, joined by another wave, then another, the crowd on its feet, unwilling to go home.

Taking it all in I thought about the time an interviewer asked me, How do you rate yourself with other comedians? I told him the best. He started laughing. The one-time laughter was not what I wanted to hear. "You think that's funny," I said. "Hey, man, if you see someone selling more tickets than me, bring him to me."

And here I am. Looking out at more than 2,500 fans. When the noise finally dies I bow my head and raise my right arm. Then I shout: *"Thank you, San Antonio!"*

And the crowd erupts once more.

When it was all over, Robin Tate, who has been in the business a long time and promoted the "Kings of Comedy" tour, nearly knocked me over backstage.

"I have never, in twenty-eight years," he said, "heard a sound like that."

You know the sounds I love the most?

The ones that arrive long after the laughter has gone and I'm signing autographs or posing for pictures backstage or in the lobby. Words from a woman who hugs me and says I give Latinos "encouragement" and how, during her treatments for cancer, my words inspired her here and here . . . pointing to head and heart.

Or the little boy with terminal cancer holding his mother's hand. His mom tearing up as she opens up and tells me how her son is constantly tormented by his classmates at school if for no other reason than his Latino last name.

"Give me a hug," I tell the boy, who does just that, hard. Then bending down, I look him in the eye.

"Don't let this stuff bother you," I say. "Do you understand me? Look at me. Think of me when they're saying those things to you. Stay strong."

Then I go to my dressing room, close the door, and cry.

LATINO FAST FOOD

Y ou know, nothing reflects the browning of America like fast-food restaurants. The days of the pimply-faced teenager working part-time because "I want to buy a car and I have to pay half" are gone. These days, these kids have been replaced by Latinos who believe that working at Burger King or McDonald's, or in this case, Jack in the Box, is a great place for a career. And that's a scary thought . . .

"Welcome to Yack in the Bock, can I hel you?"
"I'm sorry?"
"Welcome to Yack in the Bock, can I hel you?"
"What's going on, Brogan? Is this Jack in the Box? What the hell?"
"Sí, puto, es Yack in the Bock, can I hel you? You wan some shit?"
"I'm sorry?"
"I say you wanna sumpshin?"
"Yes, can I have a Jumbo Jack?"
"Oh, you want a Yumbo Yak."
"Um, I don't believe there's a Y in Jack."
"Quiere queso?"
"I'm sorry?"
"Se quiere queso?"
"Um, no Nintendo."

"I say do you like a shiz?"

"Oh, all right."

"Okay, you want one Yumbo Yak with queso with shiz."

"What did he say, Ryan? You worked at El Torito. What did he say?"

"Quiere papa frita?"

"Come again?"

"You wanna papa frita? I say you wanna frem frine? Frem frine. You wanna frem frine?"

"My friends are fine, thank you."

"Lookatthemenu."

"I'm sorry?"

"Lookatthemenu. What si'? Lookatthemenu. What si'?"

"What sign? Um, I'm a Capricorn. What does my sign gotta do with ordering a hamburger?"

And this is where you lose them, right here . . .

"And what kind of fountain drinks do you have?"

"Ah, cabrón."

Silence.

"One minute plee. Sergio, esta fountain drink que es eso?"

More silence.

"Fountain drink, what is? What is it? What is it? Who it is? What is? What is? What are? What are is?"

"A soda."

"Es soda? Es soda! Why you no say soda, stupid! Son of a bish! We got a soda, stupid. We got a Co-ca. We got a Pek-si."

"Pes-ki?"

"Pes-ki. We gotta Mr. Bibb. El Señor Pibb. You want orchata?"

"I don't wanna talk to the manager, fucker. I want sumthin to drink. Tell Orchata I want a large Pepsi."

"You wanna Esprite?"

"Es-prite?"

"Are you stupid? Esprite? E-S-P-R . . ."

AWARD WINNER

The 2003 Latin Grammys took place in the hot, sexy city of Miami, and for the first time it would be hosted by a hot, sexy comedian. I was taking over the reins from actor Jimmy Smits and determined to inject some heat and humor into the live two-hour show.

This would be the Latin Grammys' fourth annual show, and the producers were pulling out all the stops. *Feel The Latino* ads covered billboards and buses all over South Florida; Sears, Dodge, Dr Pepper, Chrysler, Bud Light, Clairol were advertising heavily on the show.

The afternoon before we aired live on CBS, the American Airlines Arena buzzed as nominees like Marc Anthony, Colombian rocker Juanes, the Black Eyed Peas, pop sensation Thalia, and Mexican metal-rappers Molotov rehearsed. Most important to me, you could sense the pride in the words of one of the show's producers, Emilio Estefan, the husband of superstar singer Gloria Estefan. While Emilio and I stood backstage listening to Ricky Martin rehearse, he leaned in and whispered, "We've come a long, long way, my friend."

My friend. Never would I have thought I'd hear that greeting from a man as singularly important to Latino culture. Today, after selling some seventy million records and CDs worldwide, Emilio and Gloria have branched out into record producing, ownership of restaurants, and several other businesses. Emilio laughed when I told

him he was probably banking a million dollars a minute. Funny, yes, but damn near true.

Fact was, by September 2003 I was riding pretty high as well. A year earlier I had presented on this show; now I was the host. New and exciting opportunities seemed to surface every day. My sold-out comedy tour had led to an appearance on *On the Record with Bob Costas,* which led, surprisingly, to a correspondent gig as the People's Commissioner on HBO's *Inside the NFL.* I had a new hit comedy album, *Team Leader,* and my TV show was headlining the revived TGIF lineup on ABC. And to top it off, I was on the cover of the September issue of *Hispanic* magazine. Yes, sir, all of a sudden the George Lopez Express was streaking down the tracks.

So there I was in Dressing Room A, prime-time real estate right next door to Ricky and Marc. A never-ending stream of production assistants waltzed in and out bearing flowers ("Excuse me, Mr. Lopez"), food ("If you need anything else, Mr. Lopez . . ."), and good wishes ("Mr. Lopez, Pat Riley is going to stop by"). Strangely, I wasn't worried about hosting the show. My trusted writing partner Aaron Lee was on hand and I had lined up eight ass-kicking wardrobe changes. Yes, indeed, the comic who just thirteen years earlier didn't have an agent, a manager, or a pulse was going to slide on stage in front of 18,000 people and a nationwide television audience, on another network no less, opposite an episode of my own *show.* (That just happened to rank No. 22 for the week.)

This show had been in production for more than a year and would feature a dozen live performances and about as many awards. My job was not only to pump up the crowd but also to keep the train on time. If one band decided to do another chorus or an acceptance speech blew past the blinking red light, it was up to me to bring the show back on track. Either that, or watch Producer Ken Ehrlich have a heart attack. Tonight, Ken told me, I would have less than a minute's leeway. That's how close they were cutting it.

Aaron and I spent much of the afternoon slicing and dicing the script, playing the jokes and punch lines out loud, discarding some—

"*You've heard of José Millionaire, he tells you he's rich but he lives at home*—while trying to retool others: *You know, we're the largest minority in America. That's 39 million Latinos—in two apartments in Hialeah!*"

I rolled joke after joke around my tongue a few dozen times, speeding some up, slowing some down, reaching for just the right cadence until even Ron, who as usual we had abused all day long—*I don't tell you what restaurant has the best senior dining, you don't tell me how to do my material; I don't tell you where to buy Depends, you don't tell me . . .* —liked what he heard. By then it was time to turn off the computer, shut the door, and focus on the show at hand.

By the time nine P.M. rolled around, Hispanic Hollywood was out in force. And I was on the air, cigar in hand, strutting down a street in South Beach.

"*Tonight I get to host the Latin Grammys. I haven't been this excited since I had Salma Hayak's name tattooed on the small of my back . . . The Latin Grammys is the hottest party and we chose Miami to hold it in—now why is that? Isn't this area known for sinister criminal activity? Like the 2000 presidential election?*"

At this point, now on the dance floor of a pulsating nightclub, I turn to the cameras: "*The Fourth Annual Latin Grammys is on the air! SHOWW!*"

After the opening tribute to Celia Cruz ends, I'm ready to rock: "*We're here in Miami and we're live and just for tonight everyone is Latino, even the people watching at home . . . so get your blood pressure checked. Don't worry, tomorrow your credit will be returned to your original good condition, and the car on blocks in your front yard will magically disappear.*"

Off and running we go, all fine through the first clothes change. Then I come out of a commercial wearing legendary Miami Dolphins quarterback Dan Marino's number thirteen game jersey. "*Tonight, we should make Dan Marino an honorary Latino. So, Dan, you'll probably get pulled over on your way home tonight. Cuidado. This is what Miami is all about. Not that CSI Miami David Caruso. That red-haired son of a bitch wouldn't last ten seconds in this heat.*"

From then on all I can think of is *keep the train-running, keep changing those clothes:* tan suit, Cuba B.C. (Before Castro) T-shirt, sailing right along until Juanes wins again, for album of the year, and one of his producers decides to give a rather windy acceptance speech. In the span of one award we'd gone from ninety seconds under to ten seconds over.

"Something's got to go," said Ehrlich.

"No, it doesn't," I said. "Don't worry. I've got it."

Fix it, George. That was my job. Fix it. Bring us back on time. Cut, trim, belch, fart, whatever you need to do, do it. So during my next two clothing changes—a righteous black suit with red accents and Caron Butler's Miami Heat jersey—Aaron and I cut and trimmed. Despite the shortened leash I got off a couple of great shots:

"It's my honor to introduce the group they call Le Madre de Toda las Bandas, which if you're in Montana means the Mother of All Bands. But if you're in Montana, you've probably changed the channel already.

"Arnold Schwarzenegger just called. He's trying to recall me as host. Arnold Schwarzenegger will never be governor of California. Because Latinos will never vote for someone who speaks worse English than we do. Hasta la vista, pendejo."

Soon after, I took complete control. I dropped a final joke, compressed the final intro, and moved into a short and sweet good-bye— *"This is a good Latino party, not like the ones we have where they hide the liquor"*—before introducing the final group, which led us, like clockwork, to the credits.

"The Billy Crystal of the Grammys!" Producer Ehrlich shouted backstage. Actually, I was feeling more like Nolan Ryan of the Houston Astros having just flamed my way to a freakin' no-hitter. Not only had I handled the show and entertained a tough crowd, half of whom barely understood English, I'd also fired three four-letters words in Spanish right past a certain dumbstruck censor.

The next day "A High Note" headline at the top of *The Miami Herald* pretty much summed up the night. Indeed, Miami had sparkled with a star-studded show. I couldn't have cared less about a

mixed review in the paper, praised in one place, criticized in another for some "dismally flat" jokes and for "spewing" *Scarface* and cutting up at Latino expense. The guy closed his review by predicting because the Latin Grammys aren't mainstream, it was likely *buenas noches* for the telecast on U.S. television.

Well, sorry to disappoint ya, bub, but when the ratings came out a few days later we'd upped our previous number by 33 percent, and from what I'd heard, all the blue-chip advertisers couldn't have been happier.

Buenas noches, my ass. Buenos días to a brand-new day of Latino power and pride.

Three days later I was set to step on an even bigger stage.

The Industry had gone on the hook by saying they wanted a dozen different comics to cohost the Emmys live on Fox. I was set to share the spotlight with some of the very best in the business: Garry Shandling, Jon Stewart, Darrell Hammond, Conan O'Brien, Ellen DeGeneres, Bernie Mac, Brad Garrett, Dennis Miller, Damon Wayans, Wanda Sykes, and Martin Short.

With that kind of lineup and a national television audience, it was inevitable that the fear factor backstage would be off the charts; we were going to be judged not only by those at home but also by each other. Funny? Well, let's see . . . No, yes, maybe, I'm not sure, on and on. Since most comics are one step from the funny farm to begin with, you could sense a closing of the *culo* right from the start. One stand-up star took to babbling backstage; another—ridiculously unprepared—stood surrounded by writers desperately pitching last-second bits.

Ninety seconds. That's all I had. Ninety ticks to set up the award for Best Reality Show and either hit or miss before everyone from *The Sopranos* to the cast of *Six Feet Under*—fitting, since I figured my

career would be on its way to dead and buried if I bombed in this room.

Consequently, I took this shit seriously. So seriously that Ann and I ended up in one of those husband-wife dramas better suited to Court TV. We went to trial on Saturday night after the third of three short sets I did at The Ice House, where I had gone to work on my material. And when I say work, I mean *work,* like a classroom, with notes on a stool, making sure I've got the jokes set out in order, editing and shaping and deleting material after every show.

After the third set, Ron's happy, I'm happy, and my cowriter Aaron is happy. Ann, however, is definitely *not happy.*

She argues I'm being offensive to Latinos. She starts right in on Aaron, saying he writes derogatory jokes. What got the bug in her ear were the Cubans in Miami, who were pissed off because I wasn't a Cuban and I spoke English. *Mr. Lopez, you may now address the court.*

"Listen, Ann," I say in my most civil tone, "the bullshit in Miami is separate from this. Everything we have is because of my balls-out attitude. I'm not concerned about what people think. I'm not doing my material for them."

I was resolved not to abandon my style the night before the Emmys. It's like getting cold feet before you get married.

Funny, it was a joke that woke me up the next morning. Something had been rolling around in my head all night, tossing and turning, until it came to me near dawn. So I got up and jotted it down on a hotel envelope. How I don't believe a hurricane is coming until somebody in a thong tells me.

Oh, did I mention that I gave Ann the cold shoulder when she got up?

"Morning," she had said from the bed.

"What's up?" I said, still ticked from the night before.

It pretty much stayed that way all day and into the early evening when we showed up at the Shrine Auditorium and were greeted with all kinds of TV love from the red-carpet crowd. Inside, Ann and I sat together and watched one comic after another take the equivalent of a leap off the Golden Gate Bridge.

Nobody seemed to want to take the plunge alone. Jon Stewart enhanced his act with a plasma screen; Conan did a dance number dressed in white tux and tails accompanied by the Rockettes. Others spiced up their act with impressions. Overall, nobody committed professional suicide, and I especially liked Stewart and Martin Short, who can do just about anything.

Then it was time for me to go backstage.

"Do you want me to go back there with you?" asked Ann.

"No," I joked, "you burned up your backstage pass last night."

Behind the stage, one of the first people I bumped into was Shandling, a guy I've known and liked since 1979.

"Comedy Store. Westwood. 1979. Purple windbreaker. Datsun 280-Z. Everything you owned in the hatchback," I said.

"Motherfuck," he said. "How did you remember that?"

"Because me and my friend Ernie used to follow you around and you'd be in the little bathroom tugging your hair and asking me how your ass looked."

"How does it look?"

"It looked good then," I said, "and it still looks good."

When I see Jennifer Garner, the star of *Alias,* whom I love, she smiles and says, "Good luck," and then all of a sudden I'm standing there alone, in the dark, under this steroid-sized Emmy statue, and I can see James Gandolfini, Sarah Jessica Parker, Robin Williams, and Bernie Mac. If truth be told, I was starting to get a little nervous, somewhere between anxious and a set of Depends. But just like that time I was

playing the Ford Theatre before the president, I told myself, *If you think you don't belong here, you don't belong here. This is why you spent those nights in El Paso and the time in Indy you wanted to walk home.*

And I think, *Fuck it. Now's the time. This is where the rubber meets the road.* I go out like Mike Tyson—no props, just gloves and shorts. Kill or be killed.

"Ladies and gentlemen, George Lopez."

Here we go. I'm dressed to kill in a bitchin' black tux, but instead of sauntering on stage I start to jog, to catch as much of the wave of applause as I can, to spin it around and use it to my advantage because I know I've got to get this crowd right from the start or this will be the longest ninety seconds of my life.

I'd put what I call a hurdle right at the beginning of my act— something that either works or doesn't, something to act as an indicator as to whether this too-cool crowd is ready to rock or roll over and play dead.

So I say, *"Thank you very much, we've reached the Hispanic Muslim portion of the show . . ."*

When the Shrine Auditorium breaks into laughter, the light in my head turns green and I'm off and running.

"I'm George Lopez, the Lopez you're not sick of . . .

"You know, I'm the perfect person to host this segment because I'm a huge fan of reality shows. I mean, I thought the first one—Dukes of Hazzard—*captured white people perfectly.*

"Contestants will do anything to get on reality shows. Fear Factor is not even funny anymore—just a chick in a sports bra chewing through a cricket. You know, if I'm going to eat cow intestines, they're going to be deep-fried with some chili."

I'm only about thirty seconds in and already a couple of good solid laughs. Now I hit them with a nice setup— *"White people—or as I like to call them, the amazing race"*—before launching into the first of my two-fisted flurries.

"I think reality shows need to diversify. I think the Latino audience can't relate. Meet the Folks, *what's that? We're forty-two and we still live at*

home. *Are You Hot? Of course we're hot. Apparently you haven't seen the women on Telemundo. I mean I only watch the news in Spanish now . . . I only believe a hurricane is coming if somebody in a thong is telling me.*

"*Not you, Al Roker. Relax. I don't want to see what's going on in your neck of the woods.*"

They're almost there now, almost ready to let go. They loved the thong line I'd dreamed up and the Roker dig. Yet I can sense they're still on edge, not quite willing to relax, so on the spur of the moment I play a card that only comes from thousands of hours on stage, a move that either breaks the barrier or blows up in your face. I'd used it a couple of times in the past in the clubs when the crowds were fighting me, playing hard to get, and I told them, "Okay, from now on, your job is *not to laugh.* No matter what I say, don't laugh." So naturally they start to laugh. And I tell them, "No, *don't laugh.*" Naturally, this goes on and on until the dam breaks and the whole place explodes.

Here, it was a little different. All that was needed was a bit of a blessing, confirmation that it was cool to come along for the ride.

So, rather softly, I said, "*You really want to laugh, it's okay. Don't feel bad.*"

And that was that. Went right back at 'em.

"Big Brother. *Twelve people living in a house. Aghhh . . . It's been done. You want to make it a reality show, put them in the garage.*"

I've got 'em now. Rounding third and heading home. Time for G. Lo to come out!

"*They say this year* [Orange County Dakota voice] *is the hardest* Survivor *yet. Oh, my God! I hope they survive! I want Tyler to survive! This year they throw you off a boat with nothing but the shirt on your back—that's how Latinos got here!*"

"Survivor Thailand. Survivor Australia. What about Survivor East LA? *A car full of white people driving around lost. 'Oh, MY GOD. We're NOT GOING TO SURVIVE. Hold me, DAKOTA!'*"

"*But my favorite reality show is* Extreme Makeover. *This is the best. You got to watch it. Man, they take an ugly-ass person, and in an hour, she's*

beautiful. Isn't that what a twelve-pack used to do? And if you're not familiar with me, I'm the Mexican in prime time."

So, in the end, the prime-time Mexican was right. I didn't need props or plasma or long-legged dancers. Nothing but my wits and attitude, and those three Saturday night sets that turned into ninety seconds of vintage me.

The finest moment may have been after I'd read the prompter detailing the honorees, and Robin Williams caught my eye. There he was, front and center, flashing me a big thumbs-up sign, which is a little like Tiger Woods telling you, "Hey, dude, love your length off the tee." Praise from the Master.

A few weeks later, at The Ice House, Brad Garrett told me when I was onstage he tapped Ray Romano on the shoulder and said, "This is what you do. You do what you know." That was really nice. I've known Brad a long time and I'm starting to know Ray a little bit, starting to get what I never got in the business until I got to this level:

Respect.

OTHER VOICES—ANN LOPEZ

I stand by what I said. George and I agree to disagree. I think just because jokes work does not mean they are up to the standard of George Lopez's writing. The thing is, I hold George, and those that occasionally offer help, to a very high standard. I hold George to a higher standard than he sometimes holds himself. That is one of the reasons he is so successful. In my opinion, those jokes were not the intelligent humor that George Lopez is known for. What can I say? I'm Cuban. We are a tough and opinionated people.

The next day's reviews offered complete vindication. The *Los Angeles Times* called my work one of the highlights of the night, noting my "inspired riff" on why Latinos can't relate to reality shows and my "sharp, topical humor." They even compared me to the likes of Lenny Bruce, Woody Allen, and Bob Hope. *TV Guide Online* tossed my name out as a potential single host for the show. But all of that would come Monday morning. Sunday night was reserved for hobnobbing at the smashing *ET* party at the Mondrian Hotel in West Hollywood, before closing down the HBO party at the Pacific Design Center, hanging out with Rob Lowe and Mike Myers, David Hyde Pierce and Jeff Garlin, and a hundred other stars.

It was late when I drove down Sunset Boulevard, the city all aglow. Up ahead I saw the billboard, virtually the same one dominating the corner of Forty-third and Broadway in New York's Times Square some three thousand miles away. Staring back was a larger-than-life picture of me advertising my stand-up shows at the Universal Amphitheatre. For a second I felt like I was talking to myself: *Hey, George, I'm proud of you, man, you stuck to your guns, you went with your heart, and you won.*

And I slowed and listened and looked for what seemed like a very long time.

THE ROOF

I bought the house the Olsen Twins used to live in. It needed a new roof.

So the insurance people sent me a check, and not knowing shit, I cashed it. I said, "Chinga," and started spending it: "Cabrón, vamos alle. Let's go to Cabo San Lucas, golfing, *pendejo*, let's go first class, *ese*, I got money."

So I spent about a third of the money that way. I planned on hiring some Raza, you know, some Mexican dudes who will fix it for a twelve-pack. But sure enough, the insurance guy sends a roofer to my house, the guy I'm supposed to give the check to. Ray the Roofer.

"Do you have the insur—"

"What? I didn't hear you?"

"The check."

"What check, *ese*? I don't know. I'm—sabes que, I'm, I'm—I'm, I can't comprende, loco."

Anyway, I end up giving what's left of the money to Ray, and who does Ray hire? Fifteen dudes from Mexico. They're wearing dress slacks and heels—no shirts. There's all this music and they're all up on the roof, and I don't even know how they got on the roof. There's no ladder. They're all on the side of the house, I can hear them: "Mira, get on it, *cabrón*. Get on my choulders. Get on my choulders." And they're all tied to one another. "Nombre, push this way," and they're getting lemons from the tree.

So I come home early one day because it's about 110 in the shade, and I figure I'll go check on them, make sure nobody's stuck to the shingles. Only there's nobody on the roof. "Ah, chinga, maybe the rope broke and they all fell." So I go in the backyard, and I look. Nobody.

I walk to the side of the house. Nobody.

I go to the courtyard. Nobody.

Finally, I work my way around to the pool, and there they are, all fifteen of them, having a gay old time, drinking Dos Equis, swimming in their calzones. Drinking and carrying on, and I'm just waiting and watching in the doorway.

And one guy looks at me and goes, "Hey, vato, jump in, the man's not home."

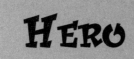

HERO

I can safely say that before me, no one in the history of my family ever swung a golf club that wasn't swung in anger.

My first club was a Spalding 7-iron. It wasn't actually mine; my grandmother kept it propped up between the garage and the backyard gate to keep the dog from pushing open the gate and running loose. As a kid, I used it to hit lemons that fell from our tree down the back alley.

My first memory of real golf was watching it on TV in the early seventies—and falling asleep. It was more of a sleeping aid than an actual sport. I'd turn it on, and immediately I'd be out.

But I knew who the guys were, like Arnold Palmer and Jack Nicklaus. I'd see their signature gear at the sporting goods stores. And, of course, Lee Trevino.

Trevino was the first Latino I ever saw play golf, and one of my great thrills recently was hanging with Lee in Dallas. On that day he was just as I always remember him; whatever he did, he did it with a smile on his face. He's still very much the Merry Mex, funny and engaging, the happiest guy of all. Think about it, a little Mexican kid who grew up dirt-poor, taught himself the game, got out of the Marines, became a golf pro, hustled and worked and won U.S. Opens and British Opens and PGA Championships. Tiger Woods is my favorite golfer, but Lee Trevino deserves a lot of credit for the changes he made for the betterment of the game.

Still, my friends and I never thought about playing golf. It was invisible. Sure, there are courses, but we never saw them; it was like a restaurant that serves food you're not into; you don't even know it's in your neighborhood until somebody points it out.

We probably had a better chance of kayaking than golfing. And the fact of the matter is that my life would have turned out very different if a golf course had not been the only place open on Christmas Day 1982.

It was about two o'clock in the afternoon, and me and Ernie were just hanging out. We'd spent the morning with our families, opened what few presents we got, and were looking for something to do. Ernie suggested we go play golf. I laughed it off.

But everything else was closed, so we drove out to this 18-hole, par-62 executive course called El Cariso in Sylmar. We rented clubs and had to give them our car keys to make sure we brought them back. Me and Ernie bought some used balls and a couple of beers and were off.

We literally did not know which club to use. We figured to hit with the biggest one first, but after our drives it was anybody's guess. There was no danger of hitting anyone, because there was nobody else on the course. It was wonderful.

I don't remember how well I hit (or didn't hit) them that day, but the thing that sticks in my mind is how it was the first time me and Ernie actually talked while we were doing something together. We were best friends and always together, but it struck me that we either did something but didn't talk, like cruising around town, or we talked but did nothing, like hanging in the backyard.

But that day, we talked the whole time, and after we were finished we sat down and talked about everything all over again. That day on the golf course deepened our friendship, and that is something I have experienced over and over again: golf brings people together and creates bonds like no other activity I've ever experienced.

I was hooked. I fell in love with the game the first time I played.

I got my first set of real clubs in 1984 in Indianapolis. I was in

town doing stand-up and met a guy at the radio station who worked at a golf store. "Give me three hundred dollars and I'll get you a set," he said. They were Wilson Dyna-Power II blades—$300 even and no receipt. Looking back, I'm guessing he carried them out the back door rather than the front.

I played steadily throughout the eighties, but it wasn't really until the early nineties that I started to take my clubs on the road. In most towns I wouldn't make it to a course; I just liked having my clubs with me. The first thing I'd do when I got into a hotel room is unpack my sticks, soak them in the toilet, and buff them with a towel. If I stayed at a place like a Residence Inn with a kitchen, I'd open up the dishwasher, dump all my golf balls in the silverware basket, and run a load to clean them.

I got so serious about the game that in 1988, with no more than $500 to my name, I went to El Cariso and dropped $250 on a set of Ping Eye2s. The good news was that I had the tools. The bad news was that I also had a temper.

When I started playing golf, I'd throw clubs and cuss and cheat—acting out all the negative shit that was going on in my life.

Finally it hit me that I really cared about this thing, this game, but I would never improve, much less succeed, if I continued disrespecting it. I came to that realization through golf, but it holds true with comedy, friendships, marriage, parenthood, everything.

Golf taught me patience, temperament, honesty, and balance. I found a focus in the game, and once I quit flinging clubs, slamming them into the turf, and fudging my score, I not only became a better golfer, I came to appreciate and enjoy the game on a level I never knew existed.

I came to liken golf to a martial art. It's rhythmic, like tai chi. Both are best done slowly because it's not about speed and strength, it's about power and precision.

My mind-set now is to laugh, have fun, and enjoy myself. I probably ought to be more focused on my shot rather than who I can make laugh or where my cigar is. At some point I should start con-

cerning myself with breaking 80, but I don't want to get to the point where I am upset because I did not shoot a certain score.

Being a celebrity golfer has its privileges. For one, you get to play courses most golfers can only wet dream about. Cypress Point on the Monterey Peninsula is one such place, right up there with Augusta National on every serious golfer's "Courses I Must Play Before I Die" list. My round at Cypress was truly unforgettable, and not just because of the spectacular design and majestic setting, but because of the company. I was graciously invited by the chef at Cypress Point, Jorge, whose benefits include a foursome a month, along with my friends RJ and Hector. For a group of Latino laborers digging an irrigation ditch, this day was no different than any other—until they saw four Mexican dudes playing golf with four white caddies. Those maintenance guys stopped, leaned on their shovels, and watched us play the entire hole, savoring the moment. And when we finished, they all raised their fists in unison in that famous show of solidarity. It looked like the closing scene from the movie *Billy Jack*.

Another perk is the latest and greatest equipment. At this year's Bob Hope Chrysler Classic Celebrity Pro-Am I reconnected with Steve Mata, a Latino brother who works as a tour rep for Titleist. PGA Tour pro David Berganio introduced me to Mata a dozen years ago when he was an underling at Taylor Made. We have both made our way to the top of our respective games, and Mata hooked me up with brand-new metalwoods, irons that are not even out on the market yet, and the white-hot Scotty Cameron Futura putter. So now I am a Titleist guy (even though I hit the snot out of my Callaway Big Bertha 5-wood!).

The driving range at a PGA Tour event is like a buffet. You can sample pretty much anything you like. One of my favorite treats is a C-Thru Grip on my putter with a picture of my bobblehead doll.

But the best part is getting to know the pros. To a man, they are nicer than I expected. Not that I expected anyone to be a jerk, but their personalities don't always come across on TV—except for John

Daly. That boy is all heart, and he wears it right on his sleeve. Those pros are out there grinding, but all the guys I have met have been great—Jesper Parnevik, Mike Weir, Charles Howell III, Aaron Baddeley, too many to mention, but most of all Vijay Singh. Talk about not coming across; that dude has a great personality and is really funny.

On second thought, getting to know the pros is the second-best thing about being a celebrity golfer. Playing in the AT&T Pebble Beach National Pro-Am is the ultimate, hands down. The prestige of the event, the setting, the history—for celebrity golfers the AT&T is our Super Bowl.

There is an added draw for me because we own a home in Pebble Beach. Our whole family can't get enough of the place. I play a ton of golf, Ann hangs out at the spa, and Mayan goes horseback riding at the equestrian center. We bought the house in February 2003 during the AT&T, which was purely coincidental, as I was not playing in the tournament.

For decades the infamous "clambake" was hosted by Bing Crosby, but today that honor belongs to Clint Eastwood, the former mayor of Carmel, current chairman of the Monterey Peninsula Foundation (which hosts the AT&T), and undisputed King of Cool.

Clint's and my offices are a chip shot apart on the Warner Bros. lot, though I had never really talked with the man until a June 2003 Latino Alliance golf tournament at Tehama, Clint's private club in Carmel. At the reception I was asked to speak, and I did a few jokes about how Clint works twenty feet from me but that I had to drive three hundred miles to say hello. The one that really broke the ice was about his wife Dina, a Latina, and how Clint thinks I am Dina's cousin Felipe from Salinas. Clint got a good laugh out of that. A while later, he saw me on HBO's *On the Record with Bob Costas* talking about how much I love golf. One thing led to another, and I got a call extending an invitation to play in the AT&T Pebble Beach Pro-Am. Imagine, a poor kid from the Valley getting invited by Clint Eastwood to play in the most prestigious pro-am in golf at Pebble Beach. It took a while

to register, and when it did I felt appreciative, humbled, and nervous as shit.

I drove up to Pebble Beach with Ann and Frank Pace the Saturday before the tournament. Frank and I played Pebble on Sunday and Poppy Hills on Monday, both days in weather that would make a mailman think twice about going outside. But the conditions are all part of the Crosby legend and the AT&T aura.

On Tuesday, the sun appeared sporadically, like a doctor popping by every so often while making rounds. I had a practice round set up with tour pro Billy Andrade, but when it came time to head down from the driving range, I couldn't get a shuttle. I didn't want to keep him waiting, so Frank shouldered my bag and we hightailed it down to the first tee.

My caddie for the week was Scott Gummer, a *Golf* magazine writer, who was doing a story about the adventure—and pleasure—of looping for me. Scott said the starter had made Billy and two other pros tee off, so he grabbed the bag from Frank and we powered out to where Billy and fellow pros Grant Waite and Tom Byrum were standing in the first fairway about to hit their second shots.

I dropped a ball near Billy's, just behind the 135-yard marker. Facing a shot that was slightly uphill and into the wind with three PGA Tour winners watching, I swung my 6-iron and held my breath. The last thing I wanted was to shank my first shot and have these guys cringe thinking I was a hack or a clown. *Plunk.* The ball stuck like a dart in the soft earth on the fringe, just inches short of the green. At which point I finally relaxed my puckered sphincter.

After the practice round I wanted to go to the pairings party to find out with which pro I'd be teamed. However, I had been asked to pay a visit to the Defense Language Institute in Monterey to talk to some of our troops. Out of respect for Clint and appreciation for the invitation, I tried to do everything that was asked of me. That's the way I am. With the show I do everything I can to help promote, pimp, market, hype, sell, and support the cause. When I do something, I do it all the way—which is the way that people with drive and ambition are typically brought up, but for me it is totally against character, because when I was growing up I didn't do shit for anybody.

As badly as I wanted to be at the pairings party, I was on a high after spending time with the troops. Things only got better when I got the call that I was paired with Jesper Parnevik.

I love this crazy Swede. First off, he freely admits that no matter what he does in the game of golf, he will never be as famous as his father, a comedian who's been called the Bob Hope of Sweden. His four adorable kids are named Peg, Penny, Phillipa, and Phoenix. He's been known to eat volcanic sand to cleanse his body. But what I love the most is Jesper's incredible flair for style, wearing wild getups like pegged pants, neon colors, wristbands (for golf?), and his trademark cap with a flipped-up bill.

If I were the Grand Poobah of Golf, I would make retro dress mandatory. No more Dockers and Polos. Golf needs to get back to the dapper days when players had style and shit, like Lloyd Mangrum and Walter Hagen.

For Wednesday's 3M Celebrity Challenge I donned some shiny gold slacks and a matching black argyle sweater. Jesper is into argyle, too, and during interviews I joked that our strategy was to nauseate the competition into submission.

The lineup for the Celebrity Challenge was stellar: Clint, Kevin Costner, Craig T. Nelson, Chris O'Donnell, Ray Romano, Kevin James, Huey Lewis, Michael Bolton, Kenny G, Clay Walker, Emmitt Smith, and me. The five-hole loop around Pebble Beach follows holes Nos. 1, 2, 3, 17 and 18. Before teeing off, we gathered on the tee for group photos facing away from the throng of fans gathered between the first tee and the pro shop. As the other guys were lining up, I was pointing my club at each of their butts, drawing howls and applause from the ladies in the crowd. Costner saw me, and as he turned around I pointed to his frontside. He blushed bright red, but that drew the biggest cheer of all.

The Celebrity Challenge format is two-man teams, alternate

shot, and my partner was Craig T., who now stars on *The District,* but everyone still calls him Coach from his years on that hit TV series. Craig T. is a solid player who carries a 5 handicap. I was playing as a 14 (which means that if he and I were playing a match, he would have to give me nine strokes—one stroke on each of the nine most difficult holes).

The Pucker Factor was definitely high as Bob Murphy, the legendary Stanford University announcer, introduced me. "From Pebble Beach, California" got a big cheer from the crowd. Not wanting to disappoint the fans or make a fool of myself, I stepped up to the tee and tried to make a nice, easy swing. I got the ball in the air and moving forward, then it started fading right. Not my best, but I was in play and the fans seemed pleased as they rewarded me with a louder cheer than my shot deserved.

This being alternate shot, the team selects the better drive, then the other guy hits the second shot. Craig T.'s drive landed in the fairway within a club length of where I had dropped the ball the previous day after catching up to Billy Andrade. I hit the 6-iron again, and again I smoothed it to the fringe just in front of the green. The gallery roared when Clint rolled in a putt for par. As I was staring down a putt to tie Clint, Bob Murphy cracked that if I wanted to be invited back, I ought to lip it out. I drilled it. I came to play, and Clint wouldn't have it any other way.

To win a hole (playing "one tie, all tie" with six teams) usually requires one person to stick an amazing shot, or a bunch of guys to all fall apart at the same time. Each of the first four holes ended in a tie, but on No. 18 Romano and James broke through for the win.

Any tensions I'd felt on the first tee had long since melted under the shining sun and warm reception I received from the fans. In homage of sorts to Bill Murray, who famously once tackled a lady spectator in a bunker, I took old Bob Murphy for a spin in the sand.

Bill Murray's absence was a hot topic all week. He was in Italy shooting a film and, try as he might, just could not make it back for the tournament. If I had a dollar for every time a reporter asked me about filling Bill Murray's comedic shoes at the AT&T, I could probably buy Pebble Beach from Clint and Arnie and their ownership group. I said it then, and I'll say it again: Bill is great, but Bill is Bill, and I am me, and there are plenty of laughs to go around.

One of the highlights of tournament week each year is the Wednesday night show for the volunteers. This ain't no little hootenanny; we're talking an audience 1,300 strong that fills the Monterey Conference Center. What's more, I didn't know what to expect from the crowd, because doing eight minutes at a variety show like this is completely different from doing my act for people who buy a ticket to come see George Lopez and know kind of what to expect from me.

I got the biggest laughs joking about buying my house in Pebble Beach.

"The day I moved in, when the moving trucks drove away, the neighbors came running out shouting, 'You forgot one! You left one behind. What about him?'"

I also got a lot of mileage that week out of bits about playing with Andy Garcia. "Andy and I are the first two Latinos to play together," I said. "They are making us wear ankle monitors. They were going to put Robert Gamez in our group, but three Latinos is a gang."

Andy's regular pro partner was Paul Stankowski, one of the most personable guys you'll ever meet. Paul and Andy won the Pro-Am a few years back, which is no small feat considering that of the 144 two-man teams (playing net best ball) that play the first three rounds, only 25 teams make the cut and play on Sunday. Just making the cut is a dream come true—just look at Jack Lemmon, who played in the tournament for over twenty-five years and never once made it to Sunday. All I wanted to do was play my game: stay out of trouble off the tee, then put myself in position to play to my strength, chipping and putting.

Our first round was Thursday morning at Poppy Hills Golf Course, and the fireworks started before we ever teed off. The driving

range was packed tighter than a carload of Chicanos on bobblehead doll day at Dodger Stadium, when the rapid-fire *click-click-click* of clubs launching balls was interrupted by the horrific collision of two players standing too close together. Heads turned to see *King of Queens* star Kevin James standing agape before his boss, CBS chairman Les Moonves, whose driver had been sliced clean off the shaft. Moonves stalked off, but as we headed to the first tee a short while later, he had a new driver in hand. If Kevin didn't pay for it that day, he might when his contract comes up.

This was my Super Bowl, and it was time to kick off. I'll admit to feeling some butterflies, but being surrounded by a big crowd did not make me as anxious as the fact that now these shots counted. I don't get nervous; I get fast. And when I swing fast I push the ball to the right, just as I did off the first tee in the Celebrity Challenge—and just as I did with my first official shot in the AT&T.

My ball squibbed short and right toward a fairway bunker. I hate the sand, but I figured to just pop it back onto the fairway, where I could play to my strength, chipping and putting. Only my ball wasn't in the sand trap. "Titleist?" asked a marshal tramping through a deep thicket. I'd missed the trap and landed in a hazard so thick I'd have needed a bazooka to shoot my ball out. My only choice was to take a penalty shot, drop my ball back in play beside the bunker, and hit again. I finally reached the green in five, then picked up when Jesper made four for par. At long last, I was playing in the AT&T—only this was not the way I had pictured it in my dreams.

Golf (like life) is a game of recovery, and the second hole at Poppy is a short par-3. Eyeing a pin that my caddie Scott had at 142 yards uphill, I took a little more club, hit my trusty 6-iron—and came up 20 yards short. Stalking off, I told Scott I didn't like the yardage, but the truth was I didn't like the shot. I did not much care for my drive into the rough off the third tee. Scott asked me, "Are you anxious?"

"I ain't anxious," I told him, "but I ain't having any fun, either."

By the fourth hole I finally settled down. I wasn't helping the team on the scorecard, but I wasn't playing myself out of holes, either. On the par-3 sixth hole, my tee shot landed just off the green in hard, tramped-down grass. The hole was cut just a couple of yards onto the green, leaving me little room to work with. But wielding my beloved 58-degree wedge, I popped the

ball up and dropped right next to the hole. "Where'd you learn that shot, George?" a fan asked. With a nod I said, "Chipping in hotel rooms."

My best line of the day came at No. 7, where I pushed my drive right, then threaded a 3-iron to the front of the green through a gap the size of a miniature golf clown's mouth. "I know how to get out of trouble," I quipped. "Been doing that my whole life!"

While Jesper made birdies at Nos. 7 and 12, I did not help the team a lick, and we finished the first round a distant 2-under par. Walking up the eighteenth fairway, Scott mentioned that he had once written a story for which he traveled to New Orleans to seek help for his golf game from a voodoo high priestess. A woman named Bloody Mary made him a good-luck gris-gris bag filled with horsehair and sassafras and all kinds of funky shit, but the next day he shot ten strokes better. "No fooling?" I asked. "You got it with you?"

Friday at Spyglass Hill Golf Course I was sporting candy apple red slacks, a white mock turtleneck, a black sweater vest, a Kangol-style hat turned backward on my head, and a voodoo gris-gris bag in my back pocket. We were the first group, starting on the back nine, and on our first hole, No. 10, I pushed my drive right but made a solid recovery to the fairway, then hit my chip stiff and rolled in a five-foot putt for par, which, with a handicap stroke, gave us a net birdie. This was more like it.

Jesper made birdie at No. 11, then at the downhill par-3 fifteenth hole I smoothed an easy 8-iron that never left the pin. The crowd started cheering before it hit the green, rolled right at the cup, and flirted with a hole-in-one but came up an inch short. I made pars for net birdies at Nos. 17 and 18 (after ricocheting my drive off a tree at

18), and at the turn we were 5-under for the round, 7-under for the tournament and feeling the groove.

While we waited to tee off on No. 1 (our tenth hole of the day), I took a new golf glove out of its bag and turned to the crowd. "Who here smokes weed?" I asked. Everyone chuckled, but nobody answered. "Anyone who is willing to step up and admit they smoke weed, I'll autograph this golf glove baggie for you." Sure enough, a guy raised his hand and stepped forward. I signed the bag, handed it to him, and said, "Now, if you get caught, you tell the cops I only gave you the bag—not what's inside!"

The first five holes at Spyglass are among the most brutal in golf. I made par/net birdie at No. 2, and Jesper drained a thirty-footer for birdie at No. 3 to get us to 9-under. I hit a solid drive at the par-4 fourth hole, leaving myself 166 yards to a pin on the lower shelf of a narrow two-tiered green. Scott and I decided I'd hit a 6-iron toward the top shelf in the hopes it would roll down. My aiming point was a fat guy in a white sweatshirt behind the green, and if I'd taken a 5-iron instead, I'd have hit that guy on the head because I flushed it absolutely pure. I knew it was good from the reaction of the crowd, a roar duplicated when I dropped the subsequent four-footer for birdie/net eagle to pick up two more strokes. Another birdie/net eagle at the par-5 seventh hole got us to 13-under for the round and, more important, back in the hunt.

Afterward we went to the driving range, and I pounded balls for hours. "Vijay who?" I joked, referring to Vijay Singh's reputation for spending hours on end on the range. "I make Vijay look lazy."

The marquee celebrity groups traditionally play Pebble on Saturday. The thinking is it helps the TV ratings, though the spectacular weather certainly wasn't hurting either. Pebble Beach is going to make big bucks off guys around the country who, trapped in their La-Z-Boys because of the snow and freezing cold, tuned in the tournament, saw Pebble awash in sunshine, and called the toll-free number during a commercial to book their dream golf vacation.

Pebble Beach really is a dreamland, and I came out firing on Sat-

urday (gris-gris bag in pocket) like I could do no wrong. I carded pars/net birdies at Nos. 1, 2, 3, 5, 6, and 9 to help get the team to 19-under. Jesper also birdied Nos. 2 and 6, but bogeyed No. 11 after I'd hit out of bounds, and we gave back a stroke—a move in the wrong direction that we could not afford.

Scott and I talked on the range that morning and figured the team needed to get to 20-under to make the cut. Now we stood at 18-under with five holes to play, none of them easy. No. 14 is rated the hardest on the course, a long, uphill par-5. A solid drive and 3-wood left me about two hundred yards out, and after talking it over I decided to play my game. Avoiding the big bunker in front of the green, I laid up and left a fifty-yard chip. The CBS guys questioned my playing safe and taking the bunker out of play, to which I replied, "I took the bunker, Salinas, Carmel, and most of Monterey out of play." But I had the last laugh when I chipped pin high to the fringe, then reclaimed a stroke by coaxing an eighteen-footer into the heart of the cup.

Nothing beats the sound of laughter—but when that crowd went from polite silence to deafening cheers in an instant, it came pretty damn close. The fans kept cheering as Jesper and I hugged then mugged for the cameras with CBS's hilarious David Feherty. "Me and Jesper, we're cornering the market on argyle," I cracked. "We're the European Starsky and Hutch."

For an encore, I rammed home another long par/net birdie putt at No. 15 and broke into a little cha-cha à la Chi Chi Rodriguez for the cameras. And with that, Jesper and I cracked 20-under. Unfortunately, it seemed a lot of other players were taking advantage of the warm weather and receptive conditions, and suddenly 20-under did not seem so safe. At No. 18, Jesper bought us a little added insurance by making birdie to get us to 21-under.

We headed for the range to work . . . and wait. It was hard to concentrate, wondering if we'd made the cut. It looked good, so much so that a number of people said we were a shoo-in, but I wasn't counting any chickens until I had a confirmed tee time Sunday

morning. Tour pro Woody Austin, who unbeknownst to me had been watching me take my cuts, suggested I move the ball slightly back in my stance so as to make contact sooner. Sure enough, the subsequent shots were sailing farther. Not alarmingly farther, but noticeably.

I took that tip (and the gris-gris bag) to the golf course with me Sunday morning. The cut wound up at 19-under. We made it. Warming up on the range, former British Open and Masters champion Mark O'Meara offered congratulations and said, "You're a player!" When he was out of earshot, I turned to Scott and whispered, "Mark O'Meara. At the Hope he said hello. Here he said, 'You're a player.' Can you believe this?"

For the final round we played in a threesome with a pro named Mark Hensby, a quiet but incredibly pleasant Australian guy who had graduated to the PGA Tour after a successful season last year on the Nationwide Tour, golf's minor league. Jesper came out blazing with birdies at Nos. 1, 2, and 4. I added a par/net birdie at No. 5. At the par-5 sixth hole, I smoked a 9-iron from a fluffy sidehill lie to within a foot and tapped in for a net eagle to get us to 27-under.

On Pebble's famously short but scenic par-3 seventh hole, I hit the exact same shot I'd hit onto the green on Saturday: a soft pitching wedge—only with the additional length I'd gained using Woody Austin's tip, my tee shot Sunday flew the green and landed in a sand trap. Jesper three-putted for bogey, I couldn't pull off a miracle, and we dropped a shot back. Jesper struggled on the back nine, and I scrambled to make a couple of pars/net birdies that got us to 28-under par. Standing on the tee at No. 16, we were six shots back with three holes to play. We were not going to win, but we were not through yet.

I made par/net birdie at No. 16, and when Jesper's putt for bird trickled home at No. 17, we reached our summit: 30-under par, a number that was absolutely beyond comprehension after finishing the first round a meager 2-under. We came to play, and we did not disappoint. And we were not disappointed. For me, just being invited

was a thrill. Making the cut was a victory in and of itself. To finish ahead of all the other celebrities and come in tied for third overall was as absurd as the prospect of a poor kid from the Valley taking up the game of golf, getting invited by Clint Eastwood to play in the AT&T . . .

The memory that still sticks with me the most came that Sunday while walking up the eighteenth fairway on the most famous finishing hole in golf. I was walking with Mark Hensby, we were taking in the moment, and we got to talking about growing up. He told me that as a boy he was told he'd never make it. I told him I didn't have a father. And yet despite our shared lack of encouragement and support, we had both made it to this place, the most hallowed ground in golf.

In golf terms, I started my life, like, 8-over par, and never got even until I was forty years old. At Pebble Beach, I went way under. On the eighteenth hole that sunny Sunday I became my own hero. I became the hero I never knew growing up.

I LOVE YOU

Ah, those three magic words.

Some dudes, man, "Oh, my God, I love you so much. Did you get my e-mail? Oh, my God. Oh, my God. I'm just so—like, oh, my God—so totally in love. I love you. Oh, my God."

But most of us? You want to start a fight, just ask this question: "Do you love me?"

"Ah, fuck, here we go. We can't even go out to eat because every time we go out you gotta start some shit."

"Do you love me?"

"I told you a long time ago I did. Pay attention. Memmer? . . . U Memmer! When you got that income tax check. Not the state, the federal."

"But do you LOVE me?"

"I'm here, ain't I? Where'm I going? All my tools are at your mom's house, I ain't going nowhere. You cosigned on the truck. I ain't going nowhere."

It seems like Latino guys are the ones with the biggest commitment issues. So what's the result? A bunch of white dudes marrying Latinas. Hey, I don't blame a Latina for being with a white dude. You know why? Because they want to be homeowners too. You stay with a Latino, you'll be renting your whole life!

"I told you, when my mom dies, we get the house! I don't know when she's going to die—ask her. Ask her."

Moms are another reason why so many white dudes are getting in. Moms love white dudes: "Oh, *mira,* he's so nice. He treats Lilly with respect. *No como loco, no shaved-head loco." Yeah, that and every time he shows up he's carrying a bottle of Crown Royal, the all-access pass to any Mexican home, even if they don't know your name:* "Ah, Crown Royal. Come in, Crown Royal. *Mira,* sit in the good chair, the one that rocks. Careful, the arm is broken."

Now, white women are different. Because when they meet our family they're just trying to fit in: "Oh, my God, do you think your mom is going to like me, like totally like me? I want her to think I rock!"

They will never like you because they don't like each other. How the hell are they going to like you?

So you stroll into the backyard barbecue, the relatives all around, holding hands with Ms. Blonde Hair. And then it starts: "Ay, *mira,* Britney Sparks *la cabrona. La* Britney Sparks. *Mira,* painted toes, *'tá loca,* painted toes, *nombre."*

Still, they want to fit in. "Oh, my God, there's your mom. Tell me again, I want your mom—how can I be a Latina?"

"I'm sorry?"

"How can I be a Latina? Tell me, how I can be a Latina?"

"You want to be a Latina? Lemme see, you wear a black bra with a white blouse. Go put lip liner on with no lipstick. Pluck your eyebrows and fuckin' pencil them back in. Yeah, that's a good start."

A Father's Day

I saved one story until the end.

It's set in Santa Barbara, on a getaway weekend for Ann and me. We're driving around town and I notice a small, brown child standing next to a makeshift lemonade stand on a quiet corner. I know that little boy, I think, standing alone on a dead-end street, always getting put down even though he's just trying to grow up and be a good boy. That's me. I pull the car over and cry for twenty minutes.

It's the little boy my therapist talked about, the one who stood alone so often, the one he said I should pretend is with me now, because it's important for that little boy to know that everything is okay, to reassure, just like I did in Austin, that I'm there for him.

Well, little boy, here is what I'd say:

Some of the pain eases every day. Take last December, for example, when I served as the Grand Marshal of a parade that began at my old elementary school and ended at my Little League field. I saw a lot of old faces and made many new friends on that ride, people in the community who were proud of what I've accomplished. Proud that I haven't forgotten where I come from. And I won't forget. Through the CARE (Community and Arts Resources for Education) Foundation, Ann and I and California state senator Richard Alarcón—the man I'm backing as the next mayor of Los Angeles—have funded grants and scholarships to help the many needy people in the San

Fernando Valley. Our efforts have ranged from buying a truck for a food bank servicing thirty thousand people a month, to assisting the Latino Theatre Company, to sponsoring leadership training for the Young Senators Program.

Still, as you know, little boy, some scars haven't healed. More and more these days I'm drawn back to the house on Hager, back to feelings defiantly complex. My grandmother is eighty-four years old now and in failing health. I don't know how much longer she'll be around. I think I'm prepared for the day she'll join my grandfather, but I'm still looking for her to say, "George, I'm so proud of you."

As my therapist once asked me, would you get mad at a blind person if he came into your home and knocked over a lamp and broke it? Of course not. The person is blind. That's Benny. She can't convey . . . she's incapable of expressing joy. Somehow, perhaps from all the pain she's endured, she sees happiness as a weakness. She doesn't see that in my show and in my act I have given her a legacy.

But you know what, little boy? Maybe I don't see all that well either. I stopped by the house on Hager with a friend recently, and he had to point out the three framed pictures carefully hung above the couch. On the left, an early publicity photo—George Lopez, Comedian—half a tube of gel lubed into my hair; in the middle, a swaggering shot of me in a tux working a club in Vegas; and on the right, the final photo: me on my wedding day, my arm around Benny, both of us all smiles. I'd never really noticed the photos before.

As I looked around the house, I saw dozens of other shots that never really clicked: in this case, Mayan, smiling at holidays, birthdays, Disneyland, Picture Day at school, while my grandmother speaks quietly, showing off my bobblehead dolls displayed on top of her TV set. I paused in front of a framed portrait of my grandfather, full of face, in his red tie, black suit, and trademark hat. And I can almost hear him saying, *I've raised you like my own son. Whatever happens, always remember me. Be a man. Be responsible.*

Proudly now, in his honor, I can honestly say I have done all three. Professionally, I'm resetting the bar almost every time out—most recently, a record 11,500 tickets for a single show in Fresno—surpassing my wildest dreams. I've become a Somebody with a show and a stand-up act—and god, is this ironic—based on humor increasingly intimate and connective. Comedy that draws people close, when for so long I used humor as a weapon to keep people away. Whereas for years I deflected any and all attempts to pierce the wall protecting my emotions, now I shoot straight for the heart.

And I've grown personally, too. From that cold, cruel house on Hager, I've walked into the warm, welcoming embrace of my wife of ten years and our eight-year-old daughter. The best nights are spent at father-daughter dances, parent-teacher conferences, or just snuggled on the couch with Ann and Mayan watching *Singin' in the Rain* and eating popcorn.

How many women, as a Valentine's Day gift, would take that old high school baseball letter tucked away in your right-hand drawer, make an exact replica of the varsity jacket your grandmother refused to buy, and present it to you after the live taping of the show? Ann did. And before the jacket was even on I broke down. Bawling my eyes out right there on Stage 4, overwhelmed by an act so thoughtful and kind, symbolic of a healthy family relationship—wife, husband, and child—I'd never known except on TV.

Some people can love right away, but I had to learn. Had to learn to love and to love back. When Mayan was first born, I would hold her. I'd pose for pictures. I even changed diapers. But I wasn't focused on her. The television would be on or I'd be doing something else. But then there was that one day when she was a little more than two months old and I stood in the doorway of her room and watched her sleep. And I realized that I was about the same age when my father left me. And I thought, *How could somebody leave and never come back? How COULD they?* Today I know that I'm already more of a father than my father ever was. I'm already better than my dad.

For the longest time, I wanted to find my father. Time and time again the incessant search for some kind of answer has served as a driving force for the show, including our 2003 season premiere when in one of those life-imitating-art moments I told Angie, "Part of me feels it's way too late to forgive him after what he's put me through. But I don't want to be angry at him the rest of my life . . . I just want to know him. That's all I ever wanted."

Yet what are the odds of tracking down a Mexican with the last name of Lopez after forty-plus years, even one with the first name of Anatasio? Especially without the benefit of DNA or a birth certificate. Remember, when my so-called father disappeared for good he took my birth certificate and some baby clothes with him. Now why is that? My sense is the dude had another family in Mexico, and wouldn't a sure free pass across the border be perfect for one of *his* kids? Then one night not long ago my grandmother revealed a secret long suspected: that another man was my father. In slow, halting words she told me she believed my father was "Guzman, a photographer." A *family* photographer, it turns out, who owned a studio in Pacoima, just up the road from Mission Hills.

According to my grandmother, Frieda spent a lot of time hanging out at this guy's house/studio in the period right before I was born. More than enough time to get pregnant, so with Ann's help I have searched for this man, this Guzman, for months now. We've checked the local phone book, photography groups, public records, hired private investigators—all to no avail.

At one point, Ann asked me, "Are you sure you want to find him?"

"You had a father, Ann," I said. "It's easy for you to say. Let me find out."

But despite our efforts I know no more about this man today than I did when I first learned his last name. I still don't know his first. And you know what? Now I agree with Ann. I don't care anymore. I've stopped looking for my dad. He was never alive, never lived in my life, not for a second, so why would I start a relationship now? What am I going to say to him? Hi, stranger. Some things are better left undone.

You see, at forty-three, I've finally learned that for so long I cried over all the *wrong* things: the absent father and distant mother; the heaping pile of thoughtless insults and abuse; the horrible self-image; the pictures never taken; the parties never thrown. How truly destructive one woman could be.

Now when I cry it's over a *family* of feelings that nobody, no matter the size of his head or color of his skin, should live without. And that's the biggest difference.

Why You Crying? No, tell me for real.

Why? Because for the first time in my long, hard life, *cabrón,* the love and laughter are *real.*

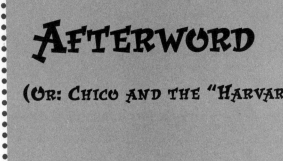

AFTERWORD

(OR: CHICO AND THE "HARVARD" MAN)

If you were sent out to search for the changing face of America, odds are the campus of Harvard University would be the last place you'd look. For most of us, Harvard conjures up ivy-covered brick buildings filled with a bunch of stiff old white dudes, Thurston Howell the Thirds and their lily-white descendants, sitting around some stuffy book-lined club, saying, "Jolly good tip on that Standard Oil stock, Jasper—and how *are* Muffy and the girls?"

Fact is, of the some 6,600 undergraduates currently enrolled at Harvard—and this is no joke, folks—34 percent are people of color. If you count foreign-born students, that number rises to nearly 40 percent.

In the words of William R. Fitzsimmons, the school's dean of undergraduate admissions, Harvard has been in the midst of "a revolution" for some time now. A cultural revolution "where people of enormous talent, people who don't need sunblock," are being welcomed and celebrated like never before in arguably the most prestigious institution of higher learning in this country.

I say all this as preamble to Saturday, February 28, 2004, without question one of the most memorable days of my life. You see, when Dean Fitzsimmons spoke further about "a role model for all of us, an inspiration to all of us here," he was standing onstage inside the historic Sanders Theatre just seconds before Dr. S. Allen Counter, chair-

man of the prestigious Harvard Foundation, would present the foundation's 2004 Artist of the Year award.

When Ron first showed me the letter marked "Confidential," I thought he was kidding. Me? A dead-end kid with a traumatic life honored as *Artist of the Year?*

By Harvard? C'mon. Let's get serious.

But then I read the letter a little more closely. Inviting me to receive Harvard's "highest performing arts and humanitarian award" for my "outstanding contributions to the performing arts" and "widely respected humanitarian contributions through the George & Ann Lopez–Richie Alarcón CARE Foundation," and, I thought, *oh my god,* these people are serious.

So it was that final weekend in February, that Ann and I and Ron and Julia Johnson from ABC traveled to Boston for what turned out to be an almost surreal experience. It began in earnest around noon on Saturday with a reception at the Kirkland House, where we were greeted not only by Professors Tom and Verena Conley, masters of the house, but by the boisterous Harvard band and a wildly diverse group of about two hundred students and faculty. After earning the distinction of doing the first *vato* pose in Kirkland House history, we were treated to a series of dead-on skits and parodies lampooning my personal and artistic life, written and performed by the students.

They had Ernie sleeping with Angie; they reprised my "hit" movie lines (lines actually spoken by Paul Rodriguez and Edward James Olmos); they had Benny with a Mexican blanket wrapped around her head, screaming about how "he probably got fired because he's a loser like his father," while, one after another, student actors dropped my signature lines—Right Now Right Now, Memmer? . . . U Memmer! Later . . . later, No Nintendo, I know, eh—perfectly into place.

After the reception we went across the hall to a wonderful lunch. From the dais I saw such hope and pride on dozens of faces, and heard Dr. Counter speak so proudly of one Latino family from a

small town in Canada that has sent five—count 'em, five—daughters to Harvard on scholarship. After listening to tributes from Martha Casillas '05, a foundation intern, and receiving gifts from the likes of Raudel Yanez '06, Harvard Raza president, it was Dr. Counter's turn. As this gentle giant of a man spoke, I could hardly believe my ears.

"I can tell you George Lopez is one of the finest individuals I have ever met, and one of the most sincere and decent people we've had here at Harvard," he said. "All of us express our deepest appreciation for your kindness, your presence, your talent, your skill, and what you represent to us."

Then it was time for Dr. Counter to introduce one of his oldest and dearest friends, David L. Evans, a sharecropper's son who went to Harvard on a scholarship funded by a founding member of Time Inc. A brilliant engineer and funny enough to give me a run for my money, David is now senior admissions officer at Harvard College. Since moving into admissions in 1970, David has been the driving force of diversity on campus; it's primarily through his efforts that Harvard has opened its mind and halls to people of color. So I took David's closing remarks to heart. Again, I could barely believe what I was hearing.

"I would like to say to George and Ann, thank you for coming, and I compare you, George, to Will Rogers and Bill Cosby, two persons who have very, very talented skills with comedy but see the big picture," he began. "They were very consequential in affecting our society for the good. You are in that same league. You're also one of the few persons who still reach what some sociologists have called the unreachable. And you do it so well. So I am glad that you made contact with Harvard students, and I hope you students will stay in contact with George and Ann, if we are going to do in this, the twenty-first century, what Martin Luther King and César Chávez and others did in the twentieth century. History will be unkind to you if they look up and say, 'When Chávez and King got out there, they still had apartheid laws in this country; they had Middle Ages farming po-

lices in this country,' but they went on anyhow, and they achieved. When you, representing the class of '07, '06, '05, and '04 . . . all of these persons, what did you do? And you won't be able to tell your grandchildren, 'Well, I had to make that payment on my Lexus.' So think of George, think of Ann, and think of being successful. You can be successful without love and you can have love without being successful. But when you put the two together and go back and look at those words again, inside those words will be the word *selfless*. And that's what he is. And that's why I wish him so well. Thank you, George."

Soon it was time to adjourn to the Sanders Theatre, where two thousand students were waiting to see me receive the Artist of the Year award and, just as important, to witness the nineteenth annual Cultural Rhythms concert that accompanies the honor.

Cultural Rhythms was the brainchild of Dr. Counter, started back in 1985 as a way for Harvard students of all ethnic and cultural backgrounds to come together and celebrate the university's increasing cultural diversity through artistic performances and culinary offerings. Today, more than forty student organizations participate in the event, sharing cultural expressions that are ethnically diverse while learning more about what connects us as people.

And I must say that what I saw on that stage over a two-hour period blew me away. All told, eighteen different groups performed, one more incredible than the next. From the '07 Steppers, sponsored by the Black Students Association, to Fuerza Latina, to Harvard Bhangra (Indian folk dance fused with some serious hip-hop), to the jaw-dropping martial arts wizardry of Harvard Wushu, to the ninety-member, bring-down-the-house gospel of the Kuumba Singers, to name but a few, I was literally, and spiritually, blown away.

What made it all the more amazing was not just the unbelievable energy, an electric current expressing pride, spirit, and talent, but the cross-pollination of virtually each and every group: Irish-Catholic and Asian-American students wearing sombreros as members of Mariachi Veritas de Harvard; white, Asian, brown, and black singing as one in Kuumba; the red-haired male stu-

dent stomping away in rubber mining boots as part of the Gumboots Dance Troupe honoring subjugated South African mine workers. Unreal. One performance after another humming with the kind of rich intercultural spirit that so many other schools, hell, much of our *society,* can only dream about.

And there I was onstage, not only witnessing it up close but being honored as a role model for what I hoped would be the next Freddie Prinze Sr. or Richard Pryor or, as David Evans stressed, the next César Chávez or Dr. King. Or maybe even me.

I thought of all that and more standing onstage, a magnificent medaled plaque from *Harvard* in hand, blinking back the tears, as the crowd stood to cheer the artist of the year.

"I didn't prepare a speech because I wanted to speak with what I have learned to do just lately—my heart. I want to tell you about a woman I have been married to for ten years, my wife, Ann, who, speaking truthfully, saved me from myself. Who saved me from destroying myself because of my background. Who saved me from wasting my life, drinking my life away, never fulfilling my dreams because of what I had come from, and truly believing and loving—truly the first person to ever truthfully, unconditionally love me.

"And I fought it. Mexican guys, we're macho, you know. She'd say 'I love you' and I'd say, *I told you I loved you already, all right. I'm here, ain't I.* . . . What I've learned from Ann is I have so much to be thankful for . . .

"I didn't expect to ever be standing in Harvard in front of Harvard people, and to all the great kids and performers here today, you are my heroes, my idea of hope and perseverance. And pride. And the fact that you are so young and so proud . . . makes an old Mexican very proud.

"And I promise you this: Being the only Latino with a show on network TV, there's a certain cachet that comes with that, and I'm going to use all of my powers for good. From this day on, thanks to you and what I've seen today, it will always be about those who I can help."

Armen's Acknowledgments

By their very nature, journeys of this kind cannot be completed alone. They require all manner of assistance, both personal and professional. With that in mind we'd like to offer our heartfelt thanks to those who, over time, often when we needed it the most, extended a helping hand and provided critical guidance and direction.

To Jack Romanos, for his belief and assistance from on high; literary agent extraordinaire Basil Kane, cool, calm and perceptive as always; Jonathon and Amy Fleming, for your beautiful retreat on Pimlico Pond and the week that made all the difference; my good friend Scott Gummer, who brought Pebble Beach, golf, and Ernie Arellano to life; consigliere Frank Pace, for insight and counsel, and for first opening the door into G. Lo's world; his assistant Karen Pagtama, always kind and efficient; Sean McManus and Tony Petitti, president and executive producer, respectively, of CBS Sports, for understanding and allowing a break from the madness of March; Ron De Blasio, who so effortlessly turns talent management into art; his able assistant, Chetan Balachandra, who simply makes things happen.

To the unwavering support from the gang at Simon & Schuster, particularly at Touchstone/Fireside: publisher Mark Gompertz; deputy publisher Chris Lloreda; publicity maven Marcia Burch; publicist Laurie Cotumaccio; production editor Martha Schwartz; and editorial assistant Ally Peltier.

To our editor, Cherise Davis, who seems to possess the rarest of

literary qualities—boundless belief and inspiration—and the capacity to continually raise the bar without injuring any of the participants, plus a voice and vision that was with us every step of the way, adding depth and texture to every page.

And finally to Ann and, most of all, George. No author could ask for better travelers or friends on this journey.